Walter Homolka (ed.)
Leo Baeck – Philosophical and Rabbinical Approaches

Aus Religion und Recht, Band 9

Walter Homolka (ed.)

Leo Baeck – Philosophical and Rabbinical Approaches

With an Introduction by Parliamentary
State Secretary Thomas Rachel

Verlag für wissenschaftliche Literatur

ISBN 978-3-86596-115-0
ISBN 3-86596-115-0
ISSN 1860-8388

© Frank & Timme GmbH Verlag für wissenschaftliche Literatur
Berlin 2007. Alle Rechte vorbehalten.

Das Werk einschließlich aller Teile ist urheberrechtlich geschützt.
Jede Verwertung außerhalb der engen Grenzen des Urheberrechtsgesetzes ist ohne Zustimmung des Verlags unzulässig und strafbar.
Das gilt insbesondere für Vervielfältigungen, Übersetzungen,
Mikroverfilmungen und die Einspeicherung und Verarbeitung in
elektronischen Systemen.

Herstellung durch das atelier eilenberger, Leipzig.
Satz: www.selignow.de
Lektorat und Redaktion: Susanne Marquardt
Printed in Germany.
Gedruckt auf säurefreiem, alterungsbeständigem Papier.

www.frank-timme.de

For Marianne C. Dreyfus
with great affection

The Abraham Geiger College is an heir to two centuries of modern Jewish studies in Germany and Europe. This volume is part of a series of theological, biblical and rabbinic studies which attempts to bring the best of modern scholarship together in symposia and the printed word. With this we seek to fulfill an intellectual obligation for the reborn Jewish community on the continent of Europe.

Contents

Preface

Thomas Rachel
Introduction: Leo Baeck – Paving the Way for a Modern Jewish Theology ... 11

Einleitung:
Leo Baeck – Geistiger Vater einer modernen jüdischen Theologie 13

Ernst Ludwig Ehrlich
Leo Baeck, der Mensch und sein Werk 19

Michael A. Meyer
„Ich bin der Ewige, Dein Gott, Du sollst!"
Das Vermächtnis Leo Baecks für das Progressive Judentum heute 37

Esther Seidel
Leo Baecks Stimme des Ausgleichs im Konflikt
zwischen liberalem Judentum und liberalem Protestantismus........... 49

Walter Homolka
Leo Baeck's Criticism on Martin Luther
and its Purpose in a Search for Jewish Identity 63

Dalia Marx
Liturgy Composed on the Brink of Catastrophe
Examination of "Akdamut Millin" by R. Meir from Worms (late 11th
century) and R. Leo Baeck's Hirtenbrief for Kol Nidre Service (1935) ... 83

Jonah Sievers
Particularism, the Other and the Question of the Burial
of Non-Jewish Spouses in a Jewish Cemetery 97

Samuel Joseph
Contemporary Challenges to Liberal Jewish Education 107

Contributors 121

Appendix:
Correspondence between Dr. Wolfgang Schäuble, Minister of the Interior of
the Federal Republic of Germany, and Marianne C. Dreyfus, Leo Baeck's
Granddaughter on the Occasion of the Fiftieth Yahrzeit of Leo Baeck.... 123

Preface

Leo Baeck (1873–1956) can be considered to be one of the most important proponents of German Jewry. Over the course of his life, he strove constantly to combine tradition and modernity within Judaism.

Baeck educated young rabbis at Berlin's "Hochschule für die Wissenschaft des Judentums" (College for the Science of Judaism) and sought dialogue between Christianity, Islam, and other religions.

Indebted to Baeck's legacy the Abraham Geiger College dedicated its annual study conference in 2006 to this brilliant Jewish thinker – to mark the fiftieth anniversary of his death on November 2, 1956. This volume celebrates the wide spectrum of Leo Baeck's heritage.

The conference was organized in co-operation with the Leo Baeck Foundation. We are very grateful for the substantial support of the German Federal Ministry of Interior for both conference and book.

Due to Susanne Marquardt this volume comes to you perfectly edited.

November 2, 2006

Rabbi Walter Homolka
Principal of the Abraham Geiger College

Thomas Rachel

Introduction: Leo Baeck – Paving the Way for a Modern Jewish Theology[*]

Leo Baeck (1873–1956) was one of the most important Jewish personalities and scholars of the past century. He was the intellectual father of modern Jewish theology in the 20th century. He studied the relationship between government and church, mainly in the Prussian state. In his view, Prussia was governed by two forces which also determined the status of Jews and Judaism: Lutheranism on the one hand and Enlightenment on the other hand. Leo Baeck championed the separation of state and church and the autonomy of every individual. Long before our time, he expressed the idea of freedom, which is now a central feature of our modern understanding of church and religion.

As Federal Chairman of the Protestant Group of the Christian Democratic Party, I know that, for some time after the establishment of the Federal Republic of Germany, Protestantism in Germany lagged far behind political Catholicism with regard to parliamentary, democratic participation and experience.

With the establishment of the Federal Republic of Germany, the situation in Germany changed along the lines of Leo Baeck's philosophy. The freedom of the churches and other religious communities, the freedom of faith and conscience and the freedom of religious or ideological belief are constitutional rights and part of everyday life in Germany today.

The relationship between the state and the churches or religious communities in Germany is determined by the requirement of separation, by religious and ideological neutrality and the secular character of the plural constitutional state. The state must be impartial and respect the religious and ideological beliefs and decisions of the holders of civil rights. But this does not mean strict separation without any relations between state and religion. State and religion interact at their interfaces.

A central point of Leo Baeck's philosophy which is still of great importance today is its respect for different beliefs and opinions and its active interest in seeking dialogue with other religions. The aim should not be to merge different religions but to ensure that people understand and respect each other. In Leo Baeck's

---

[*] This text is a summary of the speech held at an event to commemorate Leo Baeck on November 1, 2006 at the Konrad Adenauer Foundation Berlin with Rabbi Walter Homolka.

opinion, only people who have a knowledge of themselves and stand up for their own identity will be able to approach other people and enter into a dialogue with them.

Finally, Leo Baeck was very much committed to the training of young rabbis. He taught at the College for the Science of Judaism in Berlin from 1912 to 1942, when this academy was closed down. During that time, he gave new impetus to the training of rabbis. The establishment of the Abraham Geiger College in 1999 continued this tradition. The Abraham Geiger College provides training which is based on Leo Baeck's philosophy of openness, tolerance and the freedom of Jewish thinking. The first three graduates of the College were ordained as rabbis on September 14, 2006. This was the first such ordination in Germany after the holocaust. I am personally very pleased and grateful that we can now welcome a new generation of rabbis, trained in German, who distinguish themselves not only by their high standard of academic training but also by their practical and pastoral skills. The ordination in Dresden this September 2006 resumed a rich cultural and religious tradition of thinking and education which left a deep and lasting impression on intellectual life in Germany before the shoah. This ceremony shows that the Jewish tradition has its place and also a future in Germany.

Thomas Rachel

Einleitung: Leo Baeck – Geistiger Vater einer modernen jüdischen Theologie*

Leo Baeck gehört zweifelsohne zu den größten jüdischen Persönlichkeiten und Gelehrten des 20. Jahrhunderts (1873–1956). Leo Baeck war nämlich der geistige Vater einer modernen jüdischen Theologie im 20. Jahrhundert.

Als Parlamentarischer Staatssekretär des Bundesministeriums für Bildung und Forschung und als Abgeordneter des Deutschen Bundestages sind für mich die politischen Aspekte der Lehren Baecks von großem Interesse. Leo Baeck hat sich mit dem Verhältnis von Staat und Kirche vor allem im preußischen Staat befasst. Für ihn waren im preußischen Staat zwei Kräfte wirksam, die auch die Stellung der Juden und des Judentums bestimmten: das Luthertum einerseits und die Aufklärung andererseits. Leo Baeck hat sich für eine vom Staat unabhängige Kirche sowie für die Selbstständigkeit und Individualität des Menschen eingesetzt. Der Staat habe sich aus den religiösen Vollzügen seiner Bürger herauszuhalten und dürfe keinen Einfluss auf die innere Verfasstheit der Religionsgemeinschaften nehmen.

Leo Baeck hat hier – weit vor unserer Zeit – einen für unser heutiges Kirchen- und Religionsverständnis zentralen Freiheitsgedanken artikuliert.

Leo Baeck erkannte die ganze Fragwürdigkeit der Allianz von preußischem „Thron" und kirchlichem (insbesondere protestantischem) „Altar".

Zum einen war gerade die evangelische Kirche durch das preußische Königshaus (Hohenzollern) gegenüber Katholiken und anderen Religionen zwar privilegiert. Zum anderen aber waren ihr auch die Hände gebunden. Die Kirche war eben nicht frei in ihrem geistlichen Auftrag, sondern regelrecht abhängig von der weltlichen Herrschaft. Und die Kirche war gleichzeitig auch Teil des herrschaftlichen Machtapparates mit all den Fragwürdigkeiten, die das theologisch impliziert.

Leo Baeck sah dies bereits damals ganz klar. Und hier hat er über seine Zeit hinaus wegweisende Kritik und Gedanken formuliert. Dies gilt natürlich unbeschadet der Tatsache, dass man heute nicht jede Kritik, die er am Protestantismus der damaligen Zeit äußerte, teilen muss.

---

* Die Einführung beruht auf einer Rede bei der Veranstaltung zum 50. Todestag von Leo Baeck am 1. November 2006 mit Rabbiner Walter Homolka in der Akademie der Konrad-Adenauer-Stiftung in Berlin.

Für den Protestantismus in Deutschland bedeutete die Allianz von „Thron und Altar" übrigens, dass dieser – nach 1918 – in der Weimarer Republik erst ganz allmählich ein bejahendes Verhältnis zur parlamentarischen Demokratie entwickeln konnte. Als Bundesvorsitzender des Evangelischen Arbeitskreises der CDU/CSU weiß ich aus der eigenen Geschichte des EAK, wovon ich spreche: Der Protestantismus hatte noch in der jungen Bundesrepublik Deutschland gegenüber dem politischen Katholizismus einen gewaltigen Nachholbedarf in puncto parlamentarisch-demokratischer Erfahrung und Mitbestimmung.

Durchaus im Sinne von Leo Baeck haben wir nun aber seit Gründung der Bundesrepublik Deutschland eine in der deutschen Geschichte veränderte Situation. Die Unabhängigkeit der Kirchen und Religionsgemeinschaften und die Freiheit des Glaubens, des Gewissens und die Freiheit des religiösen und weltanschaulichen Bekenntnisses sind in der Verfassung garantiert und für uns selbstverständlich.

Das Verhältnis zwischen Staat und Kirche bzw. den Religionsgemeinschaften in Deutschland ist geprägt durch das Trennungsgebot, die religiös-weltanschauliche Neutralität und den säkularen Charakter des pluralistischen Verfassungsstaates. Der Staat muss die religiös-weltanschaulichen Überzeugungen und Entscheidungen der Grundrechtsträger unparteiisch respektieren und berücksichtigen. Aus diesen Geboten folgt aber keine strikte Trennung und Beziehungslosigkeit von Staat und Religion. Vielmehr wirken Staat und Religion an ihren Schnittstellen zusammen.

In Bezug auf das Christentum bedeutet das: Theologische Fakultäten und der Religionsunterricht an staatlichen Schulen zum Beispiel sind Angelegenheiten von Staat und Kirche. Sie erfüllen sowohl staatliche als auch kirchliche Funktionen. Der Staat nimmt dort seine Kulturverantwortung wahr. Er bietet außerdem institutionelle Hilfe bei der Grundrechtsverwirklichung der Religionsfreiheit. Die Kirche nutzt die theologischen Fakultäten für die Entfaltung ihrer Lehre nach wissenschaftlichen Methoden und zur Ausbildung ihres theologischen Nachwuchses. Entsprechendes gilt auch für das Judentum und die jüdische Theologie, die sich durch das segensreiche „Abraham-Geiger-Kolleg" in Deutschland auch universitär neu zu etablieren beginnt. Doch dazu komme ich gleich noch.

Wegweisend und von größter Aktualität ist das zentrale Anliegen Leo Baecks, Respekt vor dem Andersdenken zu pflegen und den Dialog mit den anderen Religionen zu suchen. Dr. Walter Homolka hat in seinen Veröffentlichungen Leo Baeck als einen Mann beschrieben, der den Respekt vor dem Andersdenken gelebt und sich entschieden für eine tolerante Haltung gegenüber den unterschied-

Einleitung: Leo Baeck – Geistiger Vater einer modernen jüdischen Theologie

lichen Richtungen des Judentums und insgesamt gegenüber anderen religiösen Überzeugungen eingesetzt hat.

Dass Toleranz dabei klare eigene Standpunkte zur Grundlage hat, bewies Leo Baeck immer wieder deutlich und damit hat er sich gerade auch um den christlich-jüdischen Dialog bleibende Dienste erworben. Das mag ein Beispiel illustrieren:

Adolf von Harnack, einer der berühmtesten und gelehrtesten protestantischen Dogmen- und Kirchenhistoriker, wollte das Alte Testament aus der christlichen Bibel entfernen haben. Für ihn war das „Alte Testament" ein Überbleibsel der jüdischen Gesetzesreligion, die durch das „Neue Testament" für ihn überholt war.

Harnack verfasste in diesem Sinne auch eines seiner berühmtesten Werke „Das Wesen des Christentums".

Dem konnte Leo Baeck selbstbewusst, profund und weitsichtig sein Werk „Das Wesen des Judentums" entgegensetzen. Insofern wirkte Harnacks Buch „Wesen des Christentums" als Katalysator für die geistige und wissenschaftliche Identifikationsfindung eines zeitgenössischen Judentums.

Leo Baeck stellte in dem wichtigen Werk richtig, dass es kein Christentum geben könne, das seine jüdischen Wurzeln zu bestreiten versucht. – Eine Erkenntnis, die für uns heute mittlerweile eine völlige theologische Selbstverständlichkeit darstellt. Aber es hat viele Jahrhunderte gebraucht, damit diese Erkenntnis auch bei uns Christen angekommen ist.

Solche Dialoge zwischen den Religionen wünscht man sich: Da unterrichtet, informiert und erinnert ein berühmter jüdischer Gelehrter seinen ebenso berühmten, christlichen Gelehrtenkollegen über dessen eigene, unaufgebbare Glaubensgrundlagen!

Ich fasse zusammen: Die Religionen sollten nicht gleich werden. Sie sollten einander verstehen und Respekt voreinander haben. Dabei war Leo Baeck der Auffassung, dass nur die Selbstkenntnis und das Bekenntnis zur eigenen Identität es möglich mache, auf den anderen zuzugehen und mit ihm ins Gespräch zu kommen.

Leo Baeck hat in seinem Geist und in seinem Wirken stets Charakter und Eigenständigkeit bewahrt. Dr. Homolka beschreibt zum Beispiel in seinem Buch „Leo Baeck: Jüdisches Denken – Perspektiven für heute", wie Leo Baeck auch in der Zeit des Nationalsozialismus bis zuletzt im Dienst des Judentums und der in Deutschland lebenden Juden blieb. Trotz der immer größer werdenden Schwierigkeiten hat er das Land nicht verlassen. Er hat sich für die Auswanderung möglichst vieler Juden, insbesondere von Kindern, eingesetzt. Noch im Konzentrationslager Theresienstadt hat er sein Wissen vom Judentum weitergegeben und mit zahlreichen Gottesdiensten und Vorlesungen versucht, seinen Mitgefangenen Mut zu machen.

Schließlich hat sich Leo Baeck sehr für die Ausbildung von Rabbinernachwuchs eingesetzt. 1912 bis zu ihrer Schließung im Jahre 1942 lehrte Baeck an der Hochschule für die Wissenschaft des Judentums in Berlin und hat dort wichtige Impulse für die Rabbinerausbildung gegeben. Mit der Gründung des Abraham Geiger Kollegs im Jahre 1999 hat man an diese Tradition angeknüpft. Die Ausbildung der Absolventen des Abraham Geiger Kollegs ist im Sinne Leo Baecks den Zielen der Offenheit, Toleranz und Freiheit des jüdischen Denkens verbunden. Im September diesen Jahres konnten die ersten drei Absolventen des Kollegs in das jüdisch-geistliche Amt des Rabbiners eingeführt wurden.

Diese Ordination ist die erste auf deutschem Boden nach dem Holocaust. Es erfüllt mich ganz persönlich mit großer Freude und Dankbarkeit, dass wir nun eine neue deutschsprachig ausgebildete Rabbinergeneration begrüßen dürfen, die sich sowohl durch ein hohes akademisches als auch praktisches und seelsorgerliches Niveau auszeichnet.

Dieses Ereignis zeigt, dass jüdisches Leben zu Deutschland gehört, einen festen Platz und eine Zukunft in diesem Land hat. Mit der Ordination wird wieder an eine segensreiche kulturell-religiöse Geistes- und Bildungstradition angeknüpft, die Deutschland in so tiefgründiger und nachhaltiger Hinsicht in der Zeit vor der Schoa intellektuell geprägt und beeinflusst hat.

Wehmütig gedenkt man dabei der schicksalsschweren Sätze Leo Baecks nach dem Kriege, als er von sich und vielen seiner Generation sagte – ich zitiere:

„Unser Glaube war es, dass deutscher und jüdischer Geist auf deutschem Boden sich treffen und durch ihre Vermählung zum Segen werden könnten. Die Epoche der Juden in Deutschland ist ein für alle Mal vorbei."

Mich bewegt in diesem Zusammenhang sehr, was der Präsident des Abraham Geiger Kollegs, Rabbiner Professor Walter Jacob, kürzlich anlässlich der ersten Rabbinerordination in Deutschland nach der Schoa sagte. Rabbiner Jacob erinnerte in bewegender Weise daran, dass 15 Generationen seiner Familie in Deutschland als Rabbiner gewirkt hatten, bevor die Nazis dieser Tradition ein jähes Ende gesetzt hatten und sagte:

„Als wir 1939 auswanderten, dachten wir nie, dass wieder jüdisches Leben entstehen würde. Mit Gottes Hilfe kam es doch dazu."

Rabbiner Dr. Walter Homolka macht sich – in der Nachfolge von Persönlichkeiten wie Leo Baeck – unter anderem als Direktor des Abraham Geiger Kollegs und als Chairman der Leo Baeck Foundation sehr um den Rabbinernachwuchs verdient. Er legt damit Zeugnis davon ab, dass zwar – wie Leo Baeck sagte – eine Epoche ein für alle Mal untergegangen ist, es aber sehr wohl neue Aufgaben, Herausforderungen und Horizonte für das Judentum in Deutschland gibt. Diese neuen Aufgaben, Herausforderungen und Horizonte eines neuen lebendigen Judentums sind ein Segen für unser Land. Sie erfüllen mich auch ganz persönlich mit großer Freude.

Der vorliegende Band zeigt, wie Rabbiner und Gelehrte des 21. Jahrhunderts anlässlich des 50. Todestags auf den berühmten Rabbiner Leo Baeck zurückblicken, der im zerrissenen Deutschland des 19. und 20. Jahrhunderts gelebt hat.

Ernst Ludwig Ehrlich

Leo Baeck, der Mensch und sein Werk

Leo Baeck, geboren am 23. Mai 1873, gestorben am 2. November 1956, kann man nicht adäquat ohne den Blick auf seine Zeit und sein Werk darstellen. Die Bedeutung seiner Persönlichkeit tritt erst ans Licht, wenn man versucht, ihn als einen der großen Lehrer des Judentums zu beschreiben, der er gewesen ist. Nur so ist auch seine Wirkung und Ausstrahlung zu verstehen und die Stärke der Erinnerung, die Menschen an ihn haben, die mit ihm zusammengetroffen sind. Daher soll hier der Versuch unternommen werden, einige Seiten seines Wesens und seiner Arbeit, seiner Leistung und seines Schicksals zu beschreiben. Alles gehört zusammen, und das Heraustrennen nur des Schicksals würde der Persönlichkeit nicht gerecht. Allein die Darstellung seiner Schriften hingegen würde nur ein unvollkommenes Bild vom Menschen vermitteln, der aus diesen Schriften auch heute noch zu uns spricht.

Seine Persönlichkeit enthielt all das, was das Beste des deutschen Judentums in sich aufgenommen und ausgedrückt hat. Wenn wir hier die Größe seiner Persönlichkeit andeuten wollen, so meinen wir damit nicht, dass er etwa einfach und geradlinig gewesen wäre, aber gerade diese Paradoxien kennzeichnen dieses eine Leben und damit auch diese geistige Epoche der Juden am Ende des 19. und in der ersten Hälfte des 20. Jahrhunderts. Leo Baeck bekannte sich zwar zum deutschen Judentum, aber er wurde 1873 in Lissa in der Provinz Posen geboren, als Nachkomme mährischer und ungarischer Juden. Posen war damals das Eingangstor zum lebendigen, pulsierenden, ungebrochenen osteuropäischen Judentum, das den Bewohnern dieser preußischen Provinz ständig vor Augen stand und das sie zugleich anzog und abstieß. Das deutsche Judentum hatte eine offene Grenze nach Osten, ein Fünftel der so genannten „deutschen Juden" hatte nicht die deutsche Staatsangehörigkeit. Kein geringer Teil der Studenten der deutschen Rabbiner kam aus Osteuropa.

Baeck wurde zwar später ein so genannter „liberaler" Rabbiner, aber er hatte in seinem Vaterhaus die jüdische Tradition in ihrem Tiefsten ernst zu nehmen gelernt, so ernst wie nur einer, der sich nicht ausdrücklich zur liberalen Richtung bekannte. Baeck war seiner ganzen geistigen Gestalt nach ein deutscher Jude, Feldrabbiner im 1. Weltkrieg, aber er hatte es stets vermieden, sich den Zweideutigkeiten dieses deutschen Judentums anzuschließen. Als einer der wenigen politischen Nichtzionisten der Zwanzigerjahre wirkte er im *Keren Hajessod*, dem

Aufbauwerk Palästinas, weil er eine tiefe Liebe zum Lande der Väter empfand. Baecks Bekenntnis zu Palästina erfolgte schon früh, früher jedenfalls als man vielleicht vermuten könnte. In dem bereits im Jahre 1917/18 in Bubers Zeitschrift „Der Jude" erschienenen Aufsatz: „Lebensgrund und Lebensgehalt" heißt es:

Man hat bisweilen draußen und drinnen gespottet über den Gedanken des freien jüdischen Hauses im Lande der Väter; aber er hat doch, wenigstens, den großen Zug, und es wäre ein großer Tag, wenn die Stätte entstünde, welche suchende Körper und suchende Seelen aufnehmen will. Ja, mag das jüdische Dasein sich in ihm betonen wie immer – wenn es nur eben ein großer Gedanke, der aus dem Engen und Kleinlichen herauszuführen vermag, um eine Zukunft zu zeigen. Wir brauchen ihn, um unseres Lebens und unseres Weiterlebens willen.[1]

Wir sprachen vorhin von den Paradoxien in Baecks Leben und Denken. Dazu gehörte auch, dass man ihn in eine Rolle gedrängt hatte, die seiner Persönlichkeit eigentlich nicht entsprach, der des so genannten „Kirchenfürsten". Was er eigentlich sein wollte, hat er auf seinen Grabstein' setzen lassen: „*mi-gesa' rabbanim*", ein Zweig in der Reihe rabbinischer Generationen, einer in der langen Kette von vielen. Ein Rabbiner war Baeck mit jeder Faser seines Seins, in einer solchen Totalität, wie nur irgendein Amtsbruder des Ostens. Hier besaß er eine sonst seltene Intoleranz gegen Berufskollegen, die nicht seinem Ethos genügten, das er für einen Rabbiner des jüdischen Volkes aufgestellt hatte. Aber er war zugleich, zumal auch für die nichtjüdische Welt, ein Grandseigneur, der Gentleman, der sich niemals einem geistigen Ghetto zugehörig fühlte und die Frömmigkeit nicht nach der Länge des Gebetmantels und der Größe des Käppchens maß. Baeck hat wie selten ein Jude vor ihm ohne jede Scheu seine kritische Haltung gegenüber christlichen Gedankengebäuden geäußert, und er war zugleich ein gerade von Christen anerkannter und gesuchter Partner im christlich-jüdischen Gespräch, das er bereits im Jahre 1901 begonnen hatte. Damals trat er auf den Plan, als er erkannte, dass Harnack in seinem Buch: „Wesen des Christentums",[2] die jüdische Wurzel des Christentums zu bestreiten versuchte. Baeck war ein Wissenschaftler, Dozent an der Lehranstalt für die Wissenschaft des Judentums in Berlin. In der Stunde der Gefahr berief man ihn an die Spitze der höchsten politischen Vertretung, die man im Jahre 1933 den Juden in Deutschland zugestand, und noch im Konzentrationslager Theresienstadt glaubten seine Mithäftlinge, den Rat des zunächst Abseitsstehenden nicht entbehren zu können.

---

[1] Leo Baeck. *Lebensgrund und Lebensgehalt*. In: *Der Jude*, Jg. 1917–1918, Heft 1–2, S. 78–86.
[2] Adolf Harnack. *Das Wesen des Christentums. 16 Vorlesungen vor Studierenden aller Facultäten im Wintersemester 1899/1900 an der Universität Berlin gehalten*. Leipzig: Hinrichs, 1900.

Baecks Lebensweg begann zunächst wie der eines begabten jungen Juden in Deutschland. Es war die Zeit, in der man eine Synthese zwischen Deutschtum und Judentum schaffen wollte, in der das Wort „und" für viele noch keine Problematik in sich zu bergen schien. Baeck hat später diese Epoche mit einem Wort Rankes gekennzeichnet: „Das Grösste, was dem Menschen begegnen kann, ist es wohl, in der eigenen Sache die allgemeine zu verteidigen." Das war der Weg der deutschen Juden in den Jahrzehnten vor dem Untergang. Versuchen wir kurz am Leben Leo Baecks diesen Weg aufzuzeigen: Studium in Breslau an der Universität und am dortigen Rabbinerseminar, das eine konservative, nicht orthodoxe Richtung aufwies. Dann, wenige Jahre später, Übersiedlung nach Berlin, wo er an der Universität und der 1872 gegründeten Lehranstalt für die Wissenschaft des Judentums studierte. 1895 Promotion bei Dilthey und Paulsen mit der Arbeit über „Spinozas erste Einwirkungen auf Deutschland".[3] Zwei Jahre später Rabbiner in Oppeln, 1907 Rabbiner in Düsseldorf, schließlich ab 1912 Rabbiner der jüdischen Gemeinde zu Berlin und Dozent an der Lehranstalt für die Wissenschaft des Judentums. Diese war nicht nur eine Rabbinerausbildungsanstalt, sondern in ihr sollte für Interessierte das weite Feld der Wissenschaft des Judentums behandelt werden.

Wir haben hier kurz Stationen eines Lebensweges verzeichnet; es muss aber noch ein Wort über die erwähnten Institutionen in Breslau und Berlin gesagt werden. Im Zuge der bürgerlichen Emanzipation der Juden und des geistigen Strebens nach den europäischen Kulturgütern entstand im 19. Jahrhundert in Deutschland die so genannte „Wissenschaft vom Judentum". Ihre vorzüglichsten Pflegestätten waren die beiden genannten Anstalten in Breslau und Berlin sowie das orthodoxe Berliner Rabbinerseminar. Was bedeutet Wissenschaft vom Judentum? Es bedeutet zunächst die Beschäftigung mit dem Judentum als Gegenstand der Wissenschaft. Das sollte an sich eigentlich selbstverständlich sein, war es jedoch nicht, da die Juden bis zum Ende des 18. Jahrhunderts auch in einem geistigen Ghetto lebten, und weder den Willen noch die Möglichkeit hatten, das Judentum wissenschaftlich, das heißt historisch-kritisch, zu erforschen. Bis zum 19. Jahrhundert hatte die wissenschaftliche Beschäftigung mit dem Judentum meist in christlichen Händen gelegen. Das ergab nicht selten eine Verzerrung des Bildes, gelegentlich aus Unkenntnis der hebräischen Quellen, gelegentlich auch aus christlich-apologetischen Motiven, wenn nicht gar aus verhülltem oder unverhülltem Antisemitismus, der dann in der Wissenschaft auch zum Antijudaismus führte. Man sah im Judentum oft nur eine Vorstufe zum Christentum (Hellenismus-Gesetz). Grätz, Frankel in Breslau, Zuns, Steinschneider und Geiger in Berlin waren die großen

---

[3] Leo Baeck. *Spinozas erste Einwirkungen auf Deutschland.* Berlin: Mayer & Müller, 1895.

Forscher jener frühen Epoche jüdischer Wissenschaft, deren geradlinige Nachfolge Baeck auf seine Art angetreten hat. Wissenschaft vom Judentum war für diese Menschen nicht ein toter Gegenstand, nicht, wie Nietzsche es einmal formuliert hat: „antiquarische Geschichte", sondern sie alle wollten mit ihrem Suchen und Forschen Antwort auf die Frage geben, die in ihnen hervorgebrochen war: Wer bist du, und wodurch bist du der geworden, der du bist, und um wessentwillen und wofür bist du es? Die Geschichte war so zu neuem Leben erwacht. Und gerade aus der Beschäftigung mit der Wissenschaft ergab sich für Baeck ein vierfaches Verständnis des jüdischen Phänomens: Geschichte, Glauben, Gerechtigkeit und Hoffnung. Hier wurde also die Modernisierung des Judentums vorgenommen. Philologie und die Edition von Texten standen anfänglich Vordergrund. Damit stellte sich auch das Problem des Geschichtlichen. In einer sich säkularisierenden Welt sollte die Wissenschaft des Judentums eine Affirmation des Jüdischen schaffen.

Die Beschäftigung mit der Geschichte zog ein sehr schwerwiegendes Problem nach sich: nämlich das der geschichtlichen Entwicklung des Judentums, ein Problem, dem strenggläubige Geister aller Religionen nicht eben wohlgesinnt sind. Darf die Offenbarung Gottes als zeitlichem Wandel unterworfen gedacht werden? Es war die Frage nach dem Substantiellen und dem Akzidentiellen, dem der Veränderung notwendig Unterworfenen. Für das Judentum war es eigentlich keine völlig neue Frage: Sie hatte sich indirekt dem alten Israel gestellt, als es in die Welt Kanaans hineingewachsen war; sie tauchte erneut auf, in der persischen, in der hellenistischen, in der römischen und in gewisser Weise auch in der arabischen Epoche. Baeck versuchte eine Antwort darauf als moderner Jude zu geben: Er erkannte, dass Starrheit Erstarrung bewirkte, Entfremdung zwischen jenen teilweise aus mythischem Denken stammenden Begriffen und dem modernen, nicht mehr im mythischen Weltbild lebenden Menschen. Und so erkannte Baeck, dass in all der Vielgestaltung jüdischen Denkens, Glaubens und Erfahrens im Grunde zwei Gedanken das Judentum charakterisieren: Das Eintreten des einen Gottes in die Welt der Vielheit, und das Gebot dieses einen Gottes, oder wie Baeck es formuliert:

Glauben ist kein gebotener Glaube, sondern ein gebietender Glaube. Er ist nicht ein gefordertes Fürwahrhalten, weder Orthodoxie noch Ekstase, sondern er ist die Wahl des Standortes und damit des Weges: ‚So Du willst, wahrst Du das Gebot; Glauben ist, Seinen Willen zu tun', wie es in dem alten jüdischen Weisheitsbuch des Jesus Sirach heißt.

Oder in einer anderen, späteren Formulierung, die sich in seinem letzten Werke findet, dessen Erscheinen er nicht mehr erlebt hat:

Der Mensch erwartet gleichsam Gott, und Gott erwartet den Menschen. Die Verheißung spricht hier, und die Forderung spricht hier, beides in einem: die Gnade des Gebotes und das Gebot der Gnade. Beides ist eines in dem einen Gotte. Um den einen Gott ist die Verborgenheit; Er offenbart sich nicht selbst, aber Er offenbart das Gebot und die Gnade, und Er, der Ewige, hat damit den irdischen Menschen eine Freiheit des Willens gegeben und ein Ziel des Willens gezeigt. Aber das Letzte bleibt dem Menschen verhüllt. Um Gott ist das Geheimnis. Er ist nicht der offenbarte Gott, aber er ist der offenbarende Gott. Und wo immer in einem Menschen die große Ehrfurcht und aus ihr erwachsend die große Bereitschaft lebt, dann ist er und dort ist er in einer Nähe zu Gott. Durch jene zwei Sätze hat dieses Volk sich zu Gott und zu sich selber bekannt: ‚Höre, Israel: Er, der ist, ist unser Gott, Er, der ist, ist Einer.' Das ist der Satz der großen Ehrfurcht, in der die Gewissheit des Glaubens wohnt. ‚Und liebe Ihn, der ist, Deinen Gott, mit Deinem ganzen Herzen und mit Deiner ganzen Seele und mit Deinem ganzen Können', das ist der Satz der großen Bereitschaft, in der sich der Mensch für Gott entscheidet. Gott ist unser Gott, das ist die Verheißung, die Gnade, in der das Gebot seinen Grund hat. Liebe Ihn, Deinen Gott, das ist das Gebot, aus dem neue Gnade wieder zuströmt. Zwei Sätze sind es, aber sie sind nicht nur Sätze, sie sind die Geschichte des Volkes.[4]

Wollen wir die Baeckschen Grundgedanken in drei Worte zusammenfassen, so können wir das mit dem Titel eines seiner wichtigsten Aufsätze aus den Zwanzigerjahren tun: „Geheimnis und Gebot."[5] Um den Begriff des Gebots kreist das gesamte Denken Baecks, ebenso wie um den des Geheimnisses. Er hat erkannt, dass jedes biblische Gebot unvollständig ist, jedes „Du sollst" seinen eigentlichen Sinn verliert, wenn man den ihm nachfolgenden Satz nicht beachtet, der lautet: „So spricht der Ewige." Die Ethik des Judentums hat ihre Wurzel in Gott. Das Judentum hört auf, wo sich der Mensch mit dem Geheimnis begnügt, gebotlose Religion ist nicht Judentum. Und ebenso wenig ist Judentum dort, wo sich das Gebot mit sich zufrieden gibt und es nur Gesetz ist, wo der Mensch alles gesehen zu haben meint, wenn er nur den Weg des Gesetzes sieht. In der Geschichte des Judentums hat der Weg des Gesetzes oft eine Antwort auf die Stunde geben können. Es ist die Antwort, die man in dem großen mittelalterlichen Gesetzeskodex des Schulchan Aruch findet. Aber der tief in der Tradition des Judentums wurzelnde Baeck hat zugleich erkannt, dass die Einwirkung, die der Schulchan Aruch ausübte, auch eine bedenkliche sein kann. Obwohl er das Festhalten am Judentum weitgehend erleichtert, ja in der Vergangenheit sogar ermöglicht hat, ist es doch ein Buch der Antworten, der abschließenden Bescheide. Das jüdische Volk hingegen ist ein fra-

---

[4] Leo Baeck. *Dieses Volk. Jüdische Existenz. Ein zweiter Teil.* Frankfurt/Main: Europäische Verlagsanstalt, 1957, S. 316ff.

[5] Leo Baeck. *Zwischen Geheimnis und Gebot. Klassische versus romantische Religion.* In: Leo Baeck. *Wege im Judentum. Aufsätze und Reden.* Berlin: Schocken, 1933, S. 33–48.

gendes Volk. Es ist ein Volk, vor dem, wie Maimonides gesagt hat, die Tore des Suchens und Forschens niemals verschlossen sind.

Ein Buch der abschließenden Bescheide bildet für jede Religion eine Gefahr. Die Gefahr nämlich eines rechtgläubigen Stillstands oder eines rechtgläubigen Hochmuts. Das Gefühl einer geistigen oder moralischen Saturiertheit konnte sich bisweilen einschleichen. Man mochte im Religiösen und im Geistigen meinen, angelangt zu sein. Aber Judentum ist auch nicht dort, wo der Glaube sich mit sich selber, mit dem Geheimnis begnügt, gebotlose Religion ist nicht Judentum. Von hier ergibt sich ohne weiteres Baecks Abgrenzung vom Paulinischen Christentum. Paulus hatte den Weg des Judentums verlassen, als er das „sola fide" predigte und damit zu Sakrament und Dogma gelangte. Da ihm das Geheimnis alles sein sollte, nicht nur das Verborgene sondern auch das Offenbarte, so ist es schließlich zum Sakrament und Dogma geworden. Mit dieser Auffassung hat Baeck Ärgernis bei christlichen Theologen erregt, denn er zog einen klaren Trennungsstrich zwischen dem alten Evangelium, das von dem Juden Jesus von Nazareth spricht, und der Paulinischen Predigt.

Das Evangelium, jenes alte Evangelium, das noch nicht zum Kirchlichen und zum Gegensatz gegen das Judentum überarbeitet war, gehört noch ganz in das Judentum hinein und zum Alten Testamente hin, so wie es in der Sprache des jüdischen Landes geschrieben war und in das jüdische Schrifttum hineingehört. Jesus und sein Evangelium können nur aus dem jüdischen Denken und Fühlen heraus, vielleicht ganz darum nur von einem Juden verstanden werden, ähnlich wie seine Worte in ihrem ganzen Inhalt und Klang gehört werden, nur wenn man sie in die Sprache, in der er sprach, zurückführt. Die Grenze, die das Judentum scheidet, beginnt bei der Paulinischen Predigt, dort, wo das Geheimnis nur ohne das Gebot, der Glaube nur ohne das Gesetz sein will.[6]

„Geheimnis und Gebot" stellt den Extrakt von Baecks Hauptwerk dar, das er einst als Antwort an Harnack geschrieben hatte: „Wesen des Judentums."[7] Es ist seit dem Jahre 1925 nicht mehr verändert, in mehrere Sprachen übersetzt worden und darf als klassische Selbstaussage des modernen Judentums gelten. Es ist ein Buch über den einen Gott und sein Gebot, aber auch ein Buch über die große Hoffnung, denn neben die Gedanken von der Geschichte und der Gerechtigkeit, tritt jener der Hoffnung, die Zukunft des Judentums. Denn diese hat Baeck dem Judentum immer vorbehalten, und eigentlich nur ihm allein. Da das Judentum eine Zukunft hat, so hat es auch eine Mission; Mission jedoch nicht im Sinne einer Proselyten-

---

[6] Leo Baeck. *Das Evangelium als Urkunde der jüdischen Glaubensgeschichte.* Berlin: Schocken, 1938, S. 69f.

[7] Leo Baeck. *Das Wesen des Judentums.* Berlin: Nathausen & Lamm, 1905.

macherei, wohl aber als Botschaft an die Welt, dass am Ende der Tage Gott als Einziger König über die ganze Erde sei, wie es im *Alenu*-Gebet heißt. Christlich-jüdische Zusammenarbeit verstand Baeck so, dass der jüdische Partner darin ganz und ohne jeden Kompromiss das Eigene vertritt. So scheute er sich auch nicht, vor Kreisen zu sprechen, denen Missionsabsichten gegenüber Juden nicht fremd waren. Er legte darauf Wert, bei denen, die das Judentum als überholt betrachteten, Botschaft und Bekenntnis abzulegen. In einer solchen Rede heißt es u.a.:

Judentum und jüdisches Volk sind das Mysterium. An ihnen kann man begreifen lernen, was in der Menschheit und ihrer Geschichte das Geheimnis ist. Wer aber das Mysterium ahnt, der wird nur mit Ehrfurcht vom Judentum und vom jüdischen Volk sprechen. Er wird nie meinen, im Rate des ewigen Gottes zu sitzen, er wird nicht seine kleinen, irdischen Gedanken als die Gedanken Gottes hinstellen. Er wird auch nicht, um etwas, was verübt worden ist oder verübt werden soll, zu legitimieren, von göttlichen Schöpfungsordnungen reden. Er wird sich auch nicht vermessen, wenn sich die Sünde in der Welt erhebt und ihr rohstes und erstes Verbrechen immer wieder gegen das jüdische Volk begeht, dann hochmütig lästernd zu sagen, dass Gott dieses Volk verworfen, es als Zeichen der Verdammnis hingestellt habe; wer so redet, müsste dann auch die, die für den Glauben, den er selber bekennt, verfolgt, getötet worden sind, als die von Gott Verworfenen, die Verdammten erklären. Juden mussten vieles erdulden, Märtyrer, Zeugen Gottes sind sie immer wieder geworden, und wenn die Wunden tief waren und bluteten und zuckten, so war doch eines immer nur bewiesen worden, welch satanischer Geist in den Foltermeistern und ihren Knechten gewesen ist. Man kann in der Tat nicht Jude sein, ohne den Willen zum Martyrium, ohne diesen Willen, vor den kleinen Menschen auch als Verworfene dazustehen.[8]

Es war von der Zukunft die Rede, von der Hoffnung, die neben dem Geheimnis und dem Gebot das Judentum konstituiert. Die Hoffnung des Juden erwächst aus der Gerechtigkeit, der Liebe und der Demut. Ist der Mensch Gottes Ebenbild und ist ihm aufgetragen, das Gute zu verwirklichen, dann folgt daraus, dass das Gute in der Zukunft siegen wird. Was Gott von dem Menschen verlangt, muss ausführbar sein. Die messianische Spannung des Judentums liegt im Wissen um die Verheißung und in der Erwartung der Erfüllung. Das Messianische ist die Vollendung und Erfüllung im Ringen um die Verwirklichung, die dem Gedanken eine gewichtige Botschaft an die Welt sein muss. Baeck ist hier zweifellos von einem Begründer der Neukantianischen Schule, von Hermann Cohen, beeinflusst, wie überhaupt Baecks ganze Denkstruktur Cohen ähnlich ist.

Derartige Vorstellungen über Judentum aus der Geschichte Israels her zu begründen, dienten eine Reihe historischer Arbeiten Baecks. Vor allem ist sein Büchlein über die Pharisäer zu nennen. Es gibt leider auch heute noch das Vorur-

---

[8] Leo Baeck. *Das Judentum auf alten und neuen Wegen*. In: *Judaica*, Jg. 6, Heft 2, 1950, S. 146.

teil, die Pharisäer seien Menschen oberflächlicher Religion oder, wie der Volksmund sie nennt, „Heuchler" gewesen. Baeck weist die tendenziöse Färbung dieses Begriffes und dieser jüdischen Volksbewegung zurück und zeigt die Frömmigkeit der jüdischen Lehrer auf, die sich selbst schon – längst vor der Polemik gegen sie in den Evangelien – gegen die „Gefärbten" in ihrer eigenen Mitte gewandt hatten. So heißt es in Baecks Pharisäer-Buch:

> Im Pharisäertum ist der großartige Versuch gemacht worden, die Religion ganz zur Religion des Lebens zu machen, des Lebens des Einzelnen und der Gesamtheit, damit die Religion nicht nur neben dem Menschen, neben der Gemeinschaft, neben dem Staate einhergehe. Mit dem Gedanken der Heiligkeit ist hier Ernst gemacht worden, unbedingter Ernst mit der Forderung, jeden Tag, auch den Alltag, zur Idee hinzuführen mit der Forderung, in der die Pharisäer ihre Aufgabe und ihr Recht fanden: ‚ihr sollt euch heiligen und heilig sein' – ‚ihr sollt peruschim, Abgesonderte, sein!' Der heroische Versuch ist hier unternommen worden, dem Gottesreiche den Boden zu bereiten. Der Name gehört einer Vergangenheit an; was er in seinem Gebote, das er enthält, bezeichnen wollte, ist ideale Wirklichkeit geblieben.[9]

An der Behandlung der Pharisäer in der modernen historischen und theologischen Wissenschaft kann man ersehen, ob ein Autor historisch-kritisch denken kann oder nur überkommene Vorurteile abschreibt.

In seiner Arbeit „Das Evangelium als Urkunde der jüdischen Glaubensgeschichte" versucht Baeck, die ursprünglichen jüdischen Schichten der Evangelien bloßzulegen und zu zeigen, dass Jesus noch in den weiten Rahmen des Judentums hineingehört. Erst Spätere, und hier vor allem Paulus, hätten nicht nur den Schritt aus dem Judentum vollzogen, sondern auch in entscheidender Weise das jüdische Jesusbild den eigenen Bedürfnissen angepasst. Diese Bedürfnisse ergaben sich durch das Eindringen der Heiden in die junge Christengemeinde. Ein trennendes Moment musste nun dadurch gefunden werden, dass man den Gegensatz zwischen Jesus und den Pharisäern betonte, die jüdischen Züge Jesu minderte und nicht die Lehre Jesu in den Mittelpunkt stellte, sondern eine Lehre von ihm, einen Glauben an ihn. Mit dieser jüdischen Jesusinterpretation stand Baeck nicht allein, seinen Standpunkt teilten im wesentlichen Buber und Klausner und hier hatte sich, und besonders dann in der zweiten Hälfte des 20. Jahrhunderts, ein Wandel innerhalb der jüdischen Forschung bemerkbar gemacht. Es ist eine Aufgabe für sich, dem nachzugehen. Baecks Lehrfach an der Lehranstalt für die Wissenschaft des Judentums war vor allem der Midrasch, verbunden mit der spätantiken jüdischen Religionsgeschichte.

---

[9] Leo Baeck. *Die Pharisäer.* Berlin: Scholem, 1927, S.72.

Die Arbeiten über die Pharisäer und die Evangelien stehen im großen Zusammenhang von Baecks Forschungen über den Midrasch, der rabbinischen Deutung der hebräischen Bibel. Er sah in der Haggada nicht etwa, wie man meinen könnte, eine literarische Gattung des Erzählgutes, sondern die spezifisch jüdische Ausdrucksform der weltanschaulichen Auseinandersetzung mit der Umwelt. Für ihn tritt im Judentum an die Stelle des Dogmas, beziehungsweise einer ausgearbeiteten Theologie, die Haggada, die erzählerisch-legendenhafte Deutung. Neben diesen wissenschaftlichen Arbeiten über die Religionsgeschichte Israels ist hier vor allem ein Werk zu nennen, das in mancher Beziehung vielleicht Baecks persönlichstes ist. Es sind die „Wege im Judentum", die 1933 in Berlin erschienen. Die mehr philosophischen Abhandlungen wurden für die Zeitschrift des Grafen Kayserling verfasst, in dessen Kreise Baeck versucht hat, Aufgabe und Gestalt des Judentums darzustellen. Ein Jude wird in diesen Kreis eingeladen, um über „Vollendung und Spannung", „Tod und Wiedergeburt", „Geheimnis und Gebot" zu reden. In diesem Bande ist auch ein 1932 für die Europäische Revue geschriebener Artikel, betitelt „Das Judentum", enthalten. In ihm finden wir einen Satz, der offenbar die kommende Katastrophe schon ahnen lässt:

Im Judentum ist eine Kunde aus alten Tagen, dass auch Völker und Staaten vor den Richterstuhl Gottes gerufen werden für das, was sie getan, für das, was sie versäumt, dass die Völker der Erde werden Rechenschaft ablegen müssen für das Geschick des Judentums in ihrer Mitte.[10]

Blättern wir weiter im Buche „Wege im Judentum". Es findet sich darin ein Artikel über Spinoza: „Motive in Spinozas Lehre." Baecks eigene Dissertation war Spinoza gewidmet gewesen, und ihm ist er trotz aller Verschiedenheit immer verpflichtet geblieben. Er versucht darzulegen, dass Spinozas Pantheismus notwendigerweise nicht mit der Lehre von dem einen Gott im Widerspruch zu stehen brauche. Und in einem hat sich Baeck ganz offenbar mit Spinoza verwandt gefühlt: In der Einheit zwischen dem eigenen Leben und der vertretenen Lehre. Spinozas asketische Züge sind Baeck immer vorbildlich erschienen. Das den Menschen in seinem freien Tun beschränkende Gebot soll Teil einer jeder Religion innewohnenden Askese sein, einer freiwilligen Beschränkung, um im Genuss und in der Maßlosigkeit das eine Ziel und den einen Weg nicht zu verlieren. „Sein Leben war Zeugnis für seine Lehre", so schrieb Baeck über Spinoza. Und auch Baecks Leben darf man diesen Zeugnischarakter zubilligen. Dann finden wir einen Aufsatz über Moses Mendelssohn. Er steht für das europäische Judentum der Neuzeit am Anfang. Typisch für Baeck in diesem Zusammenhang ist der Satz: „Ein bestimmter

---

[10] Leo Baeck. *Das Judentum*. In: *Europäische Revue*, 1932, S. 251ff.

Schritt ins Neue hinaus und eine konservative Zurückhaltung brauchen nicht zueinander im Widerspruch zu sein." Wir erinnern uns dabei einer häufig wiederholten Bemerkung Baecks: „Es gibt kein Judentum ohne die jüdische Tradition."

In seinem Werk „Wege im Judentum" charakterisiert Baeck Mendelssohn als Juden der Aufklärung. Als Jude war er ohne Einschränkung und ohne Zugeständnis das eine wie das andere, der europäische Philosoph und der „Stockjude". Nicht ein Kompromiss, sondern die Bildung einer neuen Persönlichkeit, eine Selbstschöpfung offenbart sich uns hier. Mendelssohn hatte den Beweis erbracht, wie der Jude, der sich treu blieb, der von seinem Judentum nicht abdankte noch von ihm etwas fortnahm, im neuen Europa aufrecht auf seinem Platz stand. Und dann legte Baeck seinen eigenen Zeitgenossen dar, was auch sie von Mendelssohn lernen können: Von ihm sollten sie lernen, dass sie dem großen Ganzen dienen, nicht indem sie ihr Innerstes und Tiefstes, den besonderen Charakter und den Wert aufgeben, begrenzen oder mindern, sondern dadurch erst, dass sie ihr Eigenstes mit seinem ganzen Reichtum in das Ganze, in den Staat, in die Menschheit einfügen. Ganz an sich festhalten und dadurch erst sich hingeben können, niemals von sich fortgehen, und dadurch es eben vermögen, aufrichtig und aufrecht in der Gemeinschaft zu stehen. Im geistigen Zusammenhang mit diesem Mendelssohn-Aufsatz steht ein anderer über Franz Rosenzweig, den großen jüdischen Religionsphilosophen aus den Zwanziger Jahren. Der Aufsatz gilt ebenso dem Gedächtnis Franz Rosenzweigs als auch vor allem einer Auseinandersetzung mit einem falsch verstandenen jüdischen Liberalismus, von dem Rosenzweig einst ausgegangen war. Der Liberalismus hatte gesiegt und wusste nun nicht mehr, wofür er eigentlich gesiegt hatte. Die scheinbar so erwiesene und so erledigte Frage nach der Bildung, und darüber hinaus nach der Religion und nach dem Judentum trat nun vor jeden hin, der nachzudenken begann, als eine neue Frage, als die zentrale Frage. Und Baeck zeigt, wie Franz Rosenzweig als Antwort auf die entscheidende Frage den Weg zum jüdischen Lernen, zur inneren Sicherheit und zur Lehre gegangen ist. Und wieder kommt Baeck, nun von einem ganz anderen Punkt her, zu der Erkenntnis, dass nur der Jude, der im Bunde Gottes lebt, innere Kraft und inneren Halt erfährt. Aus der Religion hervor wird er wahrhaft der Mensch seiner Heimat, seiner Geschichte. Auch darum hat es seine Bedeutsamkeit, dass Franz Rosenzweig, wenn er von seinem Deutschtum nachdenkend sprach, zuletzt immer von seinem Judentum gesprochen und gedichtet hat. „Wege im Judentum" heißt das Buch, das 1933 in Berlin erschien. Das Jahr kennzeichnet den Beginn des Unterganges des deutschen Judentums. Baecks Leben in den Jahren der Katastrophe ist sinnbildlich für das Leben der Judenheit seiner Zeit. Man versteht die Geistesgeschichte des Judentums nicht, ohne die Betrachtung des Schicksals des

Leo Baeck, der Mensch und sein Werk 29

jüdischen Volkes. Und es ist daher ein notwendiges Unternehmen, wenn wir hier in unserer Darstellung biographische Züge Leo Baecks erwähnen. Man pflegt ja gern, sich an den großen Gedankengebäuden Israels zu erfreuen, an jenem Buche, das Christen Altes Testament nennen, das von Israel in die ganze Welt gegangen ist, an den Lehren jüdischer Ethik, die man nicht umhin kann, auch im Talmud zu finden. Zu erwähnen sind hier auch die Geschichten der *Chassidim*, die durch Bubers Verdienst populär geworden sind und heute nicht selten die Predigten von Pfarrern zieren. Das alles aber bleibt blutleer, wenn man von den Menschen absieht, die solche Gedanken hervorgebracht haben, wenn man das Schicksal ignoriert, das sie erlitten. Wer das Werk Baecks betrachtet, hat auch sein Judenschicksal zur Kenntnis zu nehmen, man kann daher vom Biographischen nicht absehen. Baecks Schicksal war dasjenige eines Juden in Deutschland zur Zeit der nationalsozialistischen Verbrechen. Er stand an der Spitze der jüdischen Vertretung, war vor 1939 mehrmals kurz inhaftiert, musste mit ansehen, wie seine Mitarbeiter, einer nach dem andern, im Konzentrationslager verschwanden, aus dem sie nicht zurückkehrten.

Kol Nidre 1935 wurde Baeck kurze Zeit verhaftet, weil er in seiner Eigenschaft als Präsident der Reichsvertretung der Juden in Deutschland folgendes Gebet verfasst hatte und in allen Synagogen Deutschlands verlesen ließ:

In dieser Stunde steht jeder in Israel aufrecht vor seinem Herrn, dem Gott der Gerechtigkeit und der Gnade, um sein Herz dem Gebet zu öffnen. Vor Gott wollen wir unsere Wege befragen und unsere Taten nachsinnen, den Handlungen, die wir getan und solchen, die wir unterlassen. Wir wollen öffentlich unsere Sünden bekennen und den Ewigen bitten, dass er sie verzeihe und vergebe, indem wir unsere Übertretungen anerkennen, die individuellen und die allgemeinen, lasst uns die Verleumdungen und Lästerungen verachten, die gegen uns und unseren Glauben gerichtet werden. Wir wollen sie als Lügen entlarven, zu gemein und bedeutungslos, als dass wir sie zählen.

Gott ist unsere Zuflucht. Lasst uns Ihm vertrauen, unsere Quelle der Würde und des Stolzes. Danket dem Ewigen und preiset Ihn für unser Schicksal, für die Ehre und die Beharrlichkeit, mit der wir ausgehalten und Verfolgungen überlebt haben.

Unsere Geschichte ist die Geschichte der Größe der menschlichen Seele und der Würde des menschlichen Lebens. An diesem Tage der Sorge und des Schmerzes, umgeben von Niedertracht und Schande, wollen wir unsere Augen in die Vergangenheit richten. Von Generation zu Generation hat Gott unsere Väter erlöst, und Er wird auch uns und unsere Kinder in den Tagen, die kommen, erlösen. Wir beugen unsere Häupter vor Gott und bleiben aufrecht und gerade vor Menschen. Wir kennen unseren Weg und wir sehen den Weg zu unserem Ziel. In dieser Stunde steht das Haus Israel vor seinem Gott. Unser Gebet ist das Gebet aller Juden: unser Glaube ist der Glaube aller Juden auf Erden. Wenn wir einander ins Gesicht sehen, so wissen wir, wer wir sind, und wenn wir unsere Augen gen Himmel erheben, so wissen wir, dass die Ewigkeit mit uns ist. Denn der Hüter Israels schlummert und schläft nicht. Trauer und Elend überfließt unsere Herzen. Aufrichtig wollen wir in die tiefsten Tiefen unserer Seelen schauen, und lasst das, was nicht ausgesprochen werden kann, in das Schweigen des Nachdenkens versinken. Amen.

Dieses Dokument spiegelt eindrücklich die Situation von Juden im Jahre 1935 wider, als die Diffamierungen fortschritten und die Juden aus der Gemeinschaft des deutschen Volkes eliminiert wurden.

Baeck blieb, er blieb auf seinem Posten als Rabbiner und Dozent. Bis Juni 1942 konnte er, nun fast als einziger Dozent – jedenfalls aus dem alten Lehrerkollegium – an der Lehranstalt für die Wissenschaft des Judentums lehren. Dann wurde auch er Ende Januar 1943 verschleppt. Rückblickend schrieb er über die Zeit seiner KZ-Haft in Theresienstadt:

Manches, was in der schwarzen Zeit verübt wurde, könnte überschrieben sein: Die Bosheit als experimentatum. Ein solches Experiment des Willens zum Bösen war in ganz besonderer Weise das ausschließlich für Juden bestimmte Konzentrationslager Theresienstadt. Mit einem Minimum der Möglichkeit, gesund zu bleiben, wurde dort ein Maximum an Erkrankungsmöglichkeit verbunden; der Daseinsraum wurde durch den Sterbensraum ersetzt. Das war das Eine. In einem immer mehr verengten kleinen Bezirk wurden immer mehr Menschen hineingepresst, so dass einer am anderen sich rieb und stieß: jede Selbstsucht und Gier sollte aufwuchern und jede Anständigkeit verkümmern. Das war das Andere.

Als Baeck 1945 von den sowjetischen Truppen befreit wurde, siedelte er nach London über. Aber er blickte auf seine ehemalige deutsche Heimat. Er war sich bewusst, dass das Verhältnis der Juden zu Deutschland weder durch die Sentimentalität der Zuneigung noch derjenigen der Ablehnung bestimmt sein darf. Und er schrieb in einer deutschen Zeitschrift:

Der Jude, der sehen und hören will, sieht die Schatten, die auf sein Dasein gefallen sind, und hört die Stimme der Schatten; und es ist als würfen die Schatten noch ihre Schatten; und als sprächen auch diese. Sie sind ein Teil seines Lebens geworden. Es gibt ein Wort in der Bibel, das Gott zu Israel gesagt hat – nur Er, der Eine, durfte es sagen: ‚Ein Volk harten Nackens bist du.' Harten Nackens sind auch diese Schatten. Sie lassen sich nicht beugen und fortweisen, sie gehen mit jedem Juden und bleiben bei ihm, wenn er auf neuen Boden tritt. Verachtung ist das Gefühl, das einst die in Deutschland duldenden Juden erfasst hatte. So befremdlich es zunächst klingen mag, es gibt eine Verachtung auch für die Tüchtigkeit, und es muss sie geben können, wenn es einen Respekt vor der Tüchtigkeit geben soll. Die Entscheidung, ob jeweils das eine oder das andere zu zollen ist, zieht eine Scheidelinie zwischen Menschen.

Baeck hatte, wie manche andere Juden in Deutschland, nicht nur, um ein Wort aus dem Buche Daniel zu verwenden, den *schikkuz schomem*, den „Gräuel der Verwüstung" erlebt. Über jene deutschen Freunde, die sich bewährten, schreibt er folgendes:

Juden hatten immer wieder die Treulosigkeit erfahren, ganz unmittelbar, die Unmenschlichkeit ganz an sich selbst erduldet, und in ihrem Herzen war immer neue Bitterkeit aufgestiegen. Aber sie hatten doch auch an so manchem Tage das andere erfahren: Eine tapfere Treue, eine tapfere Liebe von dem einen und vielleicht auch dem anderen, eine menschliche Anständigkeit von einem Gekannten und einem Ungekannten. Und als sie dann hinaus gerissen wurden, haben sie wieder unter anderer Rohheit und Bosheit gelitten, deren Spur sie vielleicht noch an ihrem Körper tragen. Sie haben die einzelnen ausgesponnenen Untaten bestehen müssen. Doch immer haben sie an jene Treue einzelner und jenen Anstand einzelner gedacht. Und als sie zum Leben zurückkehrten, ist diese Erinnerung mit ihnen gegangen und zu einer Sehnsucht geworden, dankbar zu sein und zu bleiben.

Neben einzelnen Zeitschriftenaufsätzen vor allem über Probleme der Haggada sowie einer größeren Arbeit über Paulus hat Baeck sich während der letzten Jahre seines Lebens mit der Fertigstellung eines in zwei Bänden erschienen Werks beschäftigt: „Dieses Volk; Jüdische Existenz."[11] Es handelt sich dabei in seinem ersten und teilweise noch in seinem zweiten Teil um Reflexionen über die Bibel. Als Motto des ersten Bandes setzte er das Wort des Propheten Jesaja: „Dieses Volk, das Ich mir gebildet habe, meinen Ruhm wird es künden" (Jesaja 43,21). Über dem zweiten Band steht der Exodusvers: „Dieses Volk, das Du zu eigen genommen hast" (Exodus 15,16).

Über den Bund, den Auszug, die Offenbarung, Wüste und Boden handelt der erste Band. Anhand der einzelnen Stationen Israels verfolgt Baeck den Weg dieses Volkes durch die Geschichte, die er als eine Geschichte der Offenbarung erkennt. Beide Bände stellen, wenn natürlich auch nicht wörtlich, die Wiedergabe von Vorlesungen dar, die er in der langjährigen, genau 30-jährigen, Tätigkeit an der Lehranstalt gehalten hat.

Der Auszug aus Ägypten in seinem Wege und seinem Wunder ist die Einleitung zu ihr. Die Offenbarung hat dieses Volk eigentlich zu diesem Volke werden lassen, denn blieb sie ihm lebendig, so lebte das Volk in sich selber, in seinem Eigenen; das Land schließlich, das verheißene, ist das Ziel dieses Volkes, das durch die Wüste zu ihm gelangt. Die Wüste wurde zum Prägestock des Volkes, dort stand der Sinai, dort war der Offenbarung Raum gelassen und Widerhall gegeben worden. In der Wüste lenkte nichts ab, keine kanaanäische Zivilisation, keine fremden Götter. Nicht zufällig haben später die großen Propheten sich nach dieser Wüste zurückgesehnt, weil dort der Sinn für das Eigentliche geschärft worden ist: „Habt ihr etwa Opfer und Speise in der Wüste mir dargebracht die vierzig Jahre, Haus Israels", sagt Amos (Amos 5,25ff). Und dann zeichnet Baeck liebevoll und

---

[11] Leo Baeck. *Dieses Volk. Jüdische Existenz.* 2 Bde. Frankfurt/Main: Europäische Verlagsanstalt, 1955–1957.

kritisch zugleich das Bild dieses Volkes, das ewig gleiche Bild eines Volkes in der Geschichte und in der Gegenwart:

So ist dieses Volk kein glattgeschrieben Buch. Es ist ein Volk mit seiner Paradoxie und ihrer Spannung: das verbundenste und das einsamste Volk der Väter und das Volk der Kinder; das lebensfrohe und das asketische; das Volk des aufnehmenden Humors und der abweisenden Ironie, das Volk des Weges und das Volk der Hecke, das Volk, das mehr als andere nach außen und weit mehr als andere nach innen horcht und blickt, fast möchte man sagen, Volk des Landes und Volk der Wüste in einem. Es kann in dieser Paradoxie leben, weil es, und solange es in dem Glauben an das Eine und Ganze lebt. Hier ist kein wahres Fortschreiten ohne die Verbundenheit mit der Vergangenheit, keine wahre Verwobenheit mit dem Früheren, ohne den Mut zur Zukunft, keine Gewissheit ohne die Frage und keine Frage ohne die Gewissheit, kein Vertrauen ohne das Suchen und kein Suchen ohne das Vertrauen, keine Abgeschlossenheit, ohne die Erschlossenheit und keine Kraft sich zu öffnen, ohne die Fähigkeit abzulehnen.

„Wir sind fortschrittliche, liberale Juden", sagte er einmal, „nicht um des liberalen Judentums willen, sondern um des Judentums als einem großen Ganzen willen. Liberales Judentum kann seine Stärke nur inmitten des ganzen Judentums haben, inmitten kelal Jisrael. Wir wollen keine Partei sein, keine große oder kleine, sondern eine Bewegung; keine Sekte, sondern eine Kraft innerhalb des Judentums. Das liberale Judentum sollte das lebendige Gewissen des Judentums sein. Aber wir müssen auch immer wissen, dass der jüdische Standpunkt erst durch die große Geschichte geworden ist, die Geschichte der Offenbarung und des Geistes. Judentum hat seine geschichtlichen Wurzeln, es ruht auf der Tradition. Es gibt keine Tradition ohne Überzeugung, so wie es keine Überzeugung ohne die Tradition gibt. Wir Juden von heute dürfen nicht den Boden unter uns verlieren, so wie wir nicht den großen Ausblick vor unseren Augen verlieren dürfen. Tradition darf nicht zum bloßen Worte werden, denn sie steht auf einem heiligen Boden. Daher müssen wir auch für die Disziplin und sogar für die asketischen Züge der Tradition Verständnis haben, selbst Verständnis für die manchmal in Unordnung gekommene Würde der Tradition. Verständnis und Ehrfurcht sollen das Wesen des Liberalen Judentums ausmachen. Jüdisches Lernen und das Wissen um den Bund zwischen Israel und seinem Gott sind die beiden Aufgaben, die dem Judentum unserer Tage gestellt sind."

Aus diesen Worten ersieht man, dass hier nicht von einem Judentum die Rede ist, das man als ein kleines Judentum bezeichnen könnte, als ein Gebilde, das ohne den Ballast der Tradition es sich leicht machen wollte. Es ist das große Verdienst Leo Baecks gewesen, den Versuchungen des liberalen Judentums entgegengetreten zu sein, eines Judentums, das nur noch eine Karikatur gewesen wäre, in denen die Verkürzungen vorgeherrscht hätten. Jede geistige Bewegung hat ihre Gefahren, und auch innerhalb des Judentums hat es zu allen Zeiten in meist sehr ähnlicher Weise diese Gefahren gegeben. Das Grundproblem des historischen Judentums war seine geistige Schwäche, die nichts mit dem Intellekt zu tun hatte. Die geistige Schwäche, die sich vor dem großen Ausblick, vor der Schau, der Vision fürchtete, welche Angst vor der Zukunft, dem Neuen, hatte und die zu indolent war, ausgefahrene Wege zu verlassen. Das führte zur Philosophie des „als ob", als ob es noch eine Zeit gäbe, in der die alten Formen und Formeln noch ihren Sinn hätten. Die realen Tatsachen der Gegenwart wurden ignoriert, man tat so, als ob es sie nicht gäbe. Man lebte in einem luftleeren Raum. Die andere Gefahr, die sich heute im Judentum zeigt, ist nicht mehr wie im 19. Jahrhundert ein Judentum, das seine religiösen Formen der christlichen Umwelt anpasst, sondern ein religiös überhaupt entleertes Judentum. Zwei verschiedene, ja scheinbar gegensätzliche Spielarten zeigen sich hier, die beide auf eine gleiche Wurzel zurückgehen: Ein Judentum, das seine Aufgabe allein im Nationalen sieht, also ein Körper ohne Seele und Menschen jüdischer Abstammung, die nur die bloße Schicksalsgemeinschaft verbindet, vor allem also das Bewusstsein, dass sie von der nichtjüdischen Umwelt sozial nicht voll akzeptiert werden. Den religiösen Indifferentismus unserer Tage als Ergebnis der Bestrebungen der religiös-liberalen Bewegung des Judentums zu betrachten, wäre eine grobe Vereinfachung. Ihr ging es gerade darum, die echten Werte des prophetischen Judentums zu retten, ein durch Jahrhunderte der politischen Demütigung und geistigen Inzucht erstarrtes Judentum in die lebendige Gegenwart Europas einzuführen, dessen Werte also den Juden zu erschließen, ohne dabei das Eigene zu verlieren. Dieser große geistige Versuch ist gewiss oft misslungen, weil man sich einmal um das Eigene nicht klar genug war und weil man das große Ziel verlor; man wurde frei, frei aus der Knechtschaft bürgerlicher Diskriminierung, frei aus den Fesseln erstarrter Religion, die nur Praxis, nicht aber lebendiger Inhalt war. Aber man wusste dann bald nicht mehr, worin eigentlich der Inhalt bestand, welchen Weg man nach Erlangung der bürgerlichen Freiheit einzuschlagen hatte. Man zog zwar aus Ägypten aus, fand aber nicht den Weg zum Sinai, wusste nicht mehr, wo das heilige Land lag, in das man eigentlich ziehen sollte. Man hatte vergessen, wozu man auch geistig frei geworden war. Was lehrt uns nun Leo Baeck zu den Problemen, zu den Sorgen und Nöten unserer geistigen Existenz als Juden heute? Worin, so fragen wir abschließend, liegt nun die geistesgeschichtliche Bedeutung Leo Baecks? Sie liegt vor allem darin, dass er dem modernen Judentum Aufgabe und Ziel gestellt hat. Ausgegangen ist er zwar von der im 19. Jahrhundert formulierten Idee des so genannten „Ethischen Monotheismus", aber er gab dieser dürren Formel einen neuen, lebendigen Inhalt, so dass Baeck zu dem wurde, was im Judentum von jeher die Aufgabe des Rabbiners gewesen ist: Lehrer seines Volkes zu sein, denn das Judentum kennt weder den Begriff des Geistlichen, noch den des Theologen. Generationen von Schülern haben Baecks Gedankengut in alle Welt getragen und versucht, lebendiges Judentum zu gestalten. Gewiss lehrte Baeck das Primat des Ethischen, es steht auch bei ihm im Mittelpunkt, aber Ethik ist für ihn nie nur reine Spekulation gewesen, sondern Bewährung im Alltag. Im Sittlichen kann jeder Mensch Genie bewahren. Von Gott wissen und das Gute üben ist gleichbedeutend. Auserwählt zum Ärger des Philisters, diesem Gegensatz zum Gläubigen, sind die Juden als immer Unzeitgemäße nur, um die Welt zum Gottesreich zu verwandeln. So ist das Judentum für Baeck Weltreligion, denn alle können Kinder des Frommen werden. Die jüdische Religion ist nie fertig, sie ist eine dynamische Religion. Als Aufgabe weist sie dem Menschen die Entdeckung des Nächsten, des Armen, des Fremden und der Menschheit zu. Das Judentum kann nicht widerlegt werden, man kann ihm nur entgegengesetzt leben. Es ist undogmatisch, die dynamische Ethik ist auf das messianische Ziel vorwärtsgerichtet.

Aber Baeck unterscheidet sich sehr deutlich von gewissen Denkern, besonders denen des 19. Jahrhunderts, in seiner Konzeption des jüdischen Volkes und des jüdischen Landes. Sein Bekenntnis zu Israel ist auf der Geschichte gegründet, auf der Geschichte des Bundes des einen Gottes mit dem einen Volke.

„Es gibt", so schreibt er, „kaum ein zweites Beispiel solch beständiger und standhafter Treue eines Volkes gegen den Boden, auf dem seine Jugend und seine Eigenart aufgewachsen waren, kaum ein anderes Beispiel dafür, wie ein Volk körperlich von dem alten Lande getrennt, seelisch mit ihm verbunden bleibt und seelische Kraft aus ihm zieht. Es war eine Treue, die sich nicht fürchtet treu zu sein, die sich nicht scheut, im Symbol auch eine Wirklichkeit mit ihren Forderungen zu sehen, und darum in jeder Wirklichkeit ein Symbolhaftes auch, etwas, das über sie hinausweist, zu erkennen. Vielleicht ist die Treue der entscheidende Charakterzug in diesem Volke."

Und damit hat Baeck zugleich auch im Religiösen den Weg gewiesen. Es gibt im Hebräischen nicht den Begriff des Glaubens. Jenes Wort, das man gewöhnlich mit „Glauben" zu übersetzen pflegt, hat viel eher die Bedeutung: „Treue". In der Sprache Israels sind Treue, Wahrheit und Glaube ein und dasselbe Wort, sie sind untrennbar. Wahrheit und Glauben kommen aus einer Treue hervor, und alle Treue wird wieder zur Wahrheit und zum Glauben. Und lebendige Kraft steigt in ihnen auf, wenn sie aus der Treue gegen Gott aufwachsen.

Was die Aufgabe des modernen Juden ist, hat Baeck klassisch so formuliert:

Das Wissen zuerst um eine Besonderheit, um diese Gottesebenbildlichkeit durch das Persönliche. Das Bewusstsein sodann, in jedem Tage eine Antwort geben zu können, eine Antwort aus dieser Individualität hervor, diese eigene, persönliche Antwort an Gott, und das ist doch das Letzte und Tiefste aller Freiheit. Die Gewissheit schließlich, dass über allen Widersprüchen ein Ewiges ist, so dass der Mensch von Gott sein göttliches Wort, Gottes Antwort gleichsam, erwarten darf, und das ist doch das Letzte und Tiefste aller Hoffnung. Und dieses Dreifache ist in seiner Wurzel eines. Es ist die große Treue: die Treue gegen den Grund unseres Lebens, die Treue gegen das Gebot, das jeden Tag zu uns spricht, die Treue gegen das, was von uns ausgeht, was werden und weiterreichen soll. Der Bund Gottes ist hier das Prinzip, die Verbindung von Anfang und Ziel.

Fragen wir abschließend nach dem Einfluss und der Wirkung von Leo Baeck in seiner Zeit. Es dürfte in der ersten Hälfte unseres Jahrhunderts keine andere Persönlichkeit im deutschen Judentum gegeben haben, die eine ähnliche Ausstrahlung gehabt hätte wie er. Das hängt natürlich vor allem mit seiner Persönlichkeit zusammen, dann aber auch mit der Vielzahl seiner wichtigen Ämter: Gemeinderabbiner zuerst in Oppeln, dann in Düsseldorf, schließlich in Berlin; Dozent an der Lehranstalt für die Wissenschaft des Judentums; Präsident des allgemeinen deutschen Rabbinerverbandes; Präsident des deutschen Distrikts des B'nai B'rith; in Theresienstadt schließlich die Verkörperung des moralischen Gewissens. Nach dem Kriege wirkte er bis ein Jahr vor seinem Tode, 1956, am Hebrew Union College in Cincinnati. Daneben gab er regelmäßig Kurse in London für seine dorthin emigrierten ehemaligen deutschen Kollegen und Schüler. Organisatorisch hat sich Baeck auch nach dem Kriege vielfach betätigt: Als Präsident des Council of Jews from Germany, als Vorsitzender der World Union for Progressive Judaism und als Ehrenpräsident des im September 1955 gegründeten Distrikts Continental Europa des B'nai B'rith, der größten humanitären jüdischen Organisation der Welt. Wer eine derartige Fülle von Funktionen in seinem Leben in einem Zeitraum von mehr als 50 Jahren ausgeübt hat, musste Macht, Einfluss und Wirkung besitzen. Leo Baeck war sich seiner Stellung in der Welt bewusst, insbesondere auch der Anerkennung, die er bei Juden und Nichtjuden genoss. Baeck war kein Stubengelehrter, der sich aus der Politik fernhielt und sich in seine Klause zurückzog. Als der erste Band der deutschen Bibelübersetzung von Buber-Rosenzweig erscheinen sollte, dekretierte er einfach von sich aus als Präsident des deutschen B'nai B'rith, dass jedes der 12.000 Mitglieder ein Exemplar zu erwerben habe. Auf diese Weise wurde die Herausgabe dieser deutschen Übersetzung der Tora überhaupt erst möglich. Als im Jahre 1948 der Terror im damaligen Palästina herrschte, vereinte Baeck sich mit Albert Einstein in dem Appell an Juden und Araber, sich von Terror fernzuhalten, und rief die Juden auf, ein Gemeinwesen auf einer friedlichen und demokratischen Basis zu errichten. Wenn auch nicht mehr allzu viele seiner Kollegen und Schüler am Leben sind, so ist seine Botschaft an die Juden nicht vergessen. Dazu hat er doch sehr stark, gerade nach 1945, in England und in den USA gewirkt, und keine andere Gestalt im Judentum seiner Epoche hatte eine derart vielfältige Aktivität ausgeübt. Es ist im Übrigen schon ein einzigartiges Phänomen, dass er seinerzeit in Deutschland Präsident des allgemeinen Rabbinerverbandes war, obwohl er nicht der orthodoxen Richtung angehörte, diese ihn jedoch gleichwohl respektierte. Als es dann nach dem 2. Weltkrieg darum ging, aus den Trümmern des untergegangenen deutschen Judentums überall auf der Welt ein neues jüdisches Leben aufzubauen, war er wiederum führend dabei beteiligt. Einheiten der jüdischen Organisation B'nai B'rith in New York, London und Berlin tragen seinen Namen. Sie haben damit eine Verpflichtung übernommen, deren sie sich auch bewusst sind. Wir kennen daher keine andere Persönlichkeit in jener Epoche, die bis zum heutigen Tage im Bewusstsein jüdischer Menschen ist und vor allem einen Maßstab für ein Leben als Jude in Würde gesetzt hat. Nicht zuletzt trägt dazu auch das nach ihm benannte Leo Baeck Institut mit seinen Zweigstellen in New York, Jerusalem und London bei. Seine Aufgabe besteht in der Erforschung der Geschichte des deutschen Judentums, insbesondere im 19. und 20. Jahrhundert. Mit allen diesen Gremien wird der Name Leo Baecks auch in der Zukunft in steter Erinnerung derer bleiben, denen es darum geht, eine große Epoche im europäischen Judentum lebendig zu erhalten.

Michael A. Meyer

„Ich bin der Ewige, Dein Gott, Du sollst"
Das Vermächtnis Leo Baecks für das Progressive Judentum heute*

Im Jahre 1973 zum 100. Jahrestag von Leo Baecks Geburt gab Rabbi Joachim Prinz aus Livingston, New Jersey, der in Berlin mit Baeck zusammen gearbeitet hatte, ein zweiteiliges Radiointerview, das seinem Kollegen gewidmet war. Stets der Provokateur versuchte Prinz zunächst, dem Mythos von Leo Baecks Heiligenstatus einen Dämpfer zu versetzen. Nach Prinz war Baeck keinesfalls über jeden Vorwurf erhaben: er konnte zuweilen sehr schroff sein, ausweichende Antworten geben, und er war ein fürchterlicher Prediger. Aber Prinz gab auch zu, dass Baeck, obwohl er nicht über menschlichem Versagen stand, außerordentliche Qualitäten besaß, die seine Person ausmachten. Er schien all seine Kraft aus seinem Glauben zu ziehen. So war es z.B. seine Frömmigkeit, die ihm den Mut verlieh, sich zu weigern, am Sabbat vor der Gestapo zu erscheinen. Als er dann an einem Wochentag bei ihnen vorsprach, war es der Behörde unmöglich, ihn zu erniedrigen. Baeck besaß eine innere Würde, die unantastbar war. In seiner Gesellschaft, so sagte Prinz, fühlte man „die Gegenwart von Spiritualität", wie sie bei Martin Buber nicht zu spüren war.

Im Gegensatz zu Joachim Prinz, der ein Produkt der Weimarer Kultur war und deren Überschwang und laissez-faire-Haltung zusprach, war Leo Baeck ein Kind des kultivierten Zweiten Reiches. Er war zurückhaltend und verbarg sein reichhaltiges spirituelles Leben unter einem würdevollen, bisweilen distanzierten Äußeren. Sein Inneres und Äußeres waren von einem ungewöhnlichen Grad an Kohärenz geprägt. Er war eine Person wahrer Integrität.

Baeck war kein aktiver politischer Zionist, jedoch stand er dem Zionismus auch nicht ablehnend gegenüber. Auf einer Konferenz der Deutschen Liberalen Rabbiner zum Thema „Zionismus und liberales Judentum" im Jahre 1927, ergriff Baeck Partei für die jüngeren, pro-zionistischen Rabbiner und gegen seine älteren Kollegen. Er wies den Anspruch zurück, dass Zionismus, als eine säkulare Bewegung, anti-religiös sei. Ganz im Gegenteil, so stellte Baeck kühn heraus, gäbe es mehr

---

* Mit abweichendem Inhalt und in englischer Sprache wurde dieser Vortrag auch vor der Association for Progressive Judaism in New York und dem Leo Baeck College in London gehalten.

Atheisten unter den führenden liberalen Juden als unter den Zionisten. Einzigartigerweise gelang es Baeck, persona grata in beiden Lagern zu bleiben.

Gleichfalls auf religiöser Ebene unterhielt Baeck Verbindungen mit traditionelleren Juden. Aufgrund des weitläufigen Respekts, den Baeck in der jüdischen Gemeinde genoss, wurde er 1933 auserwählt, die Reichsvertretung der deutschen Juden zu leiten, die das Deutsche Judentum repräsentieren sollte. Während der nächsten 10 Jahre widmete sich Baeck, zusätzlich zu seinen Verpflichtungen als Rabbiner und Lehrer an der Hochschule für die Wissenschaft des Judentums in Berlin, der immer schwerer werdenden Aufgabe, den Kurs einer Jüdischen Gemeinde zu bestimmen, die immer bedürftiger, immer unterdrückter und immer verzweifelter wurde. Fünf mal wurde er verhaftet. Doch jedesmal legte Baeck eine Furchtlosigkeit vor den Nazis an den Tag, die dem Stereotyp des sich ängstlich duckenden Juden gänzlich widersprach.

Seine Fähigkeit, sich weder von den Einschüchterungstaktiken der Nazis, noch von der Zwietracht innerhalb der Gemeinde bezwingen zu lassen, zog er aus einer religiösen Auffassung, die er bereits in seinen jüngeren Jahren erworben hatte. Man kann, so glaube ich, von ihm sagen, dass er, mehr als jede andere jüdische Führungspersönlichkeit des 20. Jahrhunderts, seinen Glauben verinnerlicht hatte. Er verlieh ihm dann Kraft, als ein hohes Ausmaß an innerer Stärke dringend erforderlich wurde. Er wurde gänzlich seinen eigenen Prinzipien gerecht, die er schon 1928 artikulierte: „Botschaft ist nicht Predigt eines Predigers, sondern ist der Mensch selbst."

Baeck war auch ein stolzer Anhänger des Progressiven Judentums und nahm regelmäßig an den Treffen der World Union for Progressive Judaism teil. Nach dem Tod Claude Montefiores im Jahre 1938, übernahm er die Präsidentschaft und hielt sie inne, bis Lily Montagu 1955 das Amt antrat. Sein Begriff des Progressiven Judentums, so bin ich überzeugt, hat nichts von seiner Aktualität eingebüßt. Im Gegenteil, ich glaube, sich mit ihm auseinanderzusetzen, ist wichtiger denn je. In diesem Jahr, in dem Juden überall seines 50. Todestages gedenken, tun wir, die wir hier versammelt sind, gut daran, uns nicht nur an sein mutiges Leben und seine religiösen Lehren im allgemeinen zu erinnern, sondern uns auch zu fragen, welches Vermächtnis Baeck besonders uns bietet, die wir uns, wie er, progressive Juden nennen.

Der Kern von Leo Baecks religiöser Philosophie besteht aus dem bedingungslosen göttlichen Gebot, das zu tun, was recht ist. Die Zentralität des moralischen Imperativs, die Baecks Gedankengut eng mit der Philosophie Immanuel Kants verbindet, unterscheidet es von dem seines bekannteren Zeitgenossen Martin Buber. Während Bubers Gott, den er das Ewige Du nennt, in der stummen Gegenseitigkeit der Beziehung zwischen ihm und den Menschen weilt, spricht Baecks göttliches Du das menschliche Gewissen emphatisch an und fordert eine positive Antwort in der historischen Welt. Bubers Gott spricht „Du"; Baecks Gott spricht „Du sollst".

Ebenso unterscheidet sich Baecks Vorstellung der Offenbarung grundlegend von der Franz Rosenzweigs, für den Baeck großen Respekt hegte und dessen hebräische Urkunde, die ihm die „Krone des Rabbinats" verlieh, Baeck auf traditionelle Weise mit Uri Lippmann Baeck unterzeichnete. Wie Rosenzweig glaubte auch Baeck an das lebendige Gebot, das nicht auf ein Gesetz reduziert werden kann. Aber im Gegensatz zu Rosenzweig konnte Baeck Gottes fundamentales Gebot nicht als „Liebe mich" ansehen, da es den Juden, zumindest erstmal, von seinen Mitmenschen *ab*wendete, wohingegen „Du sollst" ihn anderen unmittelbar *zu*wendete.

So wie Rabbiner Abraham Geiger, nach dem dieses Kolleg benannt ist, bezog Leo Baeck seine religiöse Inspiration besonders von den hebräischen Propheten. Dem Juden, der sich an die prophetische Tradition hielt, so glaubte Baeck, ist es unmöglich, mit dem Bösen Kompromisse zu schließen. Das göttliche Gebot räumt ethischem Opportunismus keinen Platz ein. Baecks Gott gebietet; sein Gott, so schrieb er, gäbe keine Ratschläge. Der Jude ist immer zuerst seinem Gott verantwortlich und erst danach seinen Mitmenschen. Zwei Jahre, nachdem die Nazis an die Macht gekommen waren, fasste Baeck es in einer *Kol Nidre* Ansprache nachdrücklich in Worte, als er sagte:

> Wir stehen vor unserem Gott. Sein Gebot, das wir erfüllen, gibt uns Kraft. Ihm beugen wir uns, und wir sind aufrecht vor den Menschen. Ihm dienen wir, und wir bleiben fest in allem Wechsel des Geschehens.

Gehorsam gegenüber Gott, so Baeck, schließt Gehorsam gegenüber jeder weltlichen Autorität aus, die dem Willen Gottes zuwiderhandelt.

Da Gottes Gebot absolut ist, ist es selbst unter den schwierigsten Bedingungen auch immer eine unabwendbare Aufforderung zum Handeln. Heldentum ist keine Wahl, die zur Selbstverherrlichung getroffen wird. Es ist die Erfüllung einer Obligation im Angesicht von Gefahr für die eigene Person. Das Judentum, wenn es Ernst genommen wird, mag eine völlige Unterordnung der eigenen Person fordern, um das Gebot zu erfüllen. Mit Baecks Worten: „Der Heroismus ist nur das abschließende Gebot der jüdischen Religiosität, der stärkste Ausdruck ihres Ernstnehmens." Da die Ethik des Judentums unbeugsam und unerschütterlich ist und daher der Welt überlegen bleibt, kann sie fordern, dass wir unsere Seele aufs Spiel setzen, wenn die Pflicht es verlangt. In seinem letzten großen Werk, das den

Titel „Dieses Volk: Jüdische Existenz" trägt, drückte es Baeck äußerst prägnant aus: „Aus dem großen ‚Ich bin der, der ist – du sollst!' erwächst die große Furchtlosigkeit." Als Rabbiner und Vorsitzender der Reichsvertretung der deutschen Juden versuchte Baeck, diese Furchtlosigkeit, dieses Bewusstsein, dass Juden letztendlich nur ihrem Gott verantwortlich sind, in die Herzen der Juden Deutschlands einzuflößen.

In früheren Studien habe ich es schon erwähnt, dass der Ausdruck „Und dennoch" in Baecks religiöser Philosophie immer wieder auftaucht. Er nimmt in seinem Gedankengut den Platz eines Wächters gegen Opportunismus, Eigeninteresse und Verzweiflung ein. Man muss das tun, was recht ist, ungeachtet persönlicher Begehren oder Konsequenzen. Man muss an Gott glauben, auch wenn die Realität die Existenz Gottes verleugnet. Der Ausdruck erscheint auch in Baecks Briefen. Im Jahre 1939 schrieb er aus Berlin an Rabbi Max Grünewald, der wenige Monate zuvor nach Amerika ausgewandert war: „Wir hier sind weiter bemüht, im ‚Und dennoch' zu bleiben und […] das Gespenst des Chaos zu bannen." Es war seine Pflicht, so glaubte Baeck, gegen das Chaos anzukämpfen, indem er die Emigration der Juden so effizient, effektiv und fair wie möglich organisierte – eine extrem schwere Aufgabe in den späten 30er Jahren, als niemand mehr glaubte, dass die Juden eine Zukunft in Deutschland hätten und jeder Deutschland so schnell wie möglich verlassen wollte.

Weil sein in der Religion begründetes Pflichtgefühl es verlangte, führte Baeck seine Arbeit fort. Kurz vor seiner eigenen Deportation nach Theresienstadt schrieb er am 12. Dezember 1942 aus Berlin an die jüdische Dichterin Ilse Blumenthal-Weiss in Holland:

Mir selbst gehen meine Tage in der Arbeit, der oft so schweren und vergeblichen, hin. Doch sie bringt immer wieder die guten, glücklichen Augenblicke, wenn es möglich wird, Menschen zu helfen und zur Seite zu stehen.

Als die Verschleppungen aus Deutschland im Herbst 1941 ernsthaft begannen, war Baecks Aufgabe tatsächlich fast unmöglich geworden. Die Nazis kontrollierten jeden seiner Schritte und erlaubten ihm nur selten, eine unabhängige Entscheidung zu treffen. Einmal jedoch überließen sie ihm eine Entscheidung – eine, die ihn vor eine fast unmögliche Wahl stellte. Sie informierten ihn, dass das Zusammentreiben der Juden in Berlin in Kürze beginnen würde und auf zwei Arten geschehen könnte. Entweder könnten die Nazi-Behörden die zur Deportation bestimmten Juden aus ihren Häusern holen und auf einem Sammelplatz zusammentreiben, oder Baeck könnte Mitglieder der jüdischen Gemeinde dazu bestimmen, diese Aufgabe zu übernehmen. Im ersteren Falle würden die Juden zweifellos schlecht behandelt und vielleicht Gewalttätigkeiten ausgesetzt werden. Falls die Juden die Organisation übernähmen, ersparten sie den Nazis die Mühe und würden in die Nazi-Mordmaschinerie verstrickt, aber es garantierte zumindest, dass die Opfer, wenn auch nur zunächst, menschlich behandelt würden. In Anbetracht der Tatsache, dass sich die Deportationen sowieso nicht mehr aufhalten ließen, entschied sich Baeck für die zweite Alternative und übertrug die Aufgabe Deportationsbriefe auszutragen den Rabbinerstudenten des Liberalen Seminars.

Am 27. Januar 1943 wurde Baeck selbst nach Theresienstadt deportiert, wo er zweieinhalb Jahre überlebte. Zu Anfang seines Aufenthalts wurde der 69-Jährige gezwungen, einen Müllwagen durch das Lager zu ziehen. Später, nachdem er das 70. Lebensjahr erreicht hatte, befreite man ihn von dieser Aufgabe, und er begann im Lager das zu machen, was er früher als Rabbiner und Lehrer getan hatte. Er spendete Trost und versuchte denen zu helfen, die es am nötigsten hatten. Er hielt auch öffentliche Vorlesungen, die überraschend gut besucht wurden, wenn man die Hungersnot und Erschöpfung der Lagerinsassen bedenkt. Wir haben eine Liste der Themen, denen sich Baeck in diesen Vorlesungen widmete. Einige behandelten Philosophie im allgemeinen: Plato und Kant; andere jüdische Philosophen wie Maimonides, Moses Mendelssohn und Hermann Cohen. Wieder andere waren zur Jüdischen Geschichte: die Makkabäer, die Pharisäer, das mittelalterliche Ghetto, die Jüdische Aufklärung. Der außergewöhnlichste Vortrag, den er hielt, war sicherlich „Die Stellung des Arbeiters in der Jüdischen Lehre", ein Thema, das für die einst bürgerlichen deutschen Juden in Theresienstadt an Bedeutung gewonnen hatte.

Nach dem Krieg lebte Baeck in London bei seiner Tochter und unterrichtete gelegentlich am Hebrew Union College in Cincinnati. Er kehrte auch wiederholt nach Deutschland zurück, wo er im Jahre 1954 aus Anlass des 750. Todestages von Moses Maimonides eine Vorlesung hielt. Unter der großen Zuhörerschaft an diesem Tag war auch Theodor Heuss, Deutschlands erster Bundespräsident und ein Freund Baecks aus der Vorkriegszeit. Der Zweck von Baecks Vortrag lag nicht darin, Maimonides Schriften auf diese oder jene Art zu interpretieren und noch einmal die Fragen des Rambam anzusprechen, die jüdische Denker im 18. und 19. Jahrhundert beschäftigt hatten. Baecks Aussage war eine andere und dem Anlass besonders angemessen. Was er herausstellte, war, dass der mittelalterliche jüdische Philosoph und Rechtsgelehrte Maimonides seine eigene Person gewesen war. In dem Tumult seiner Zeit war es ihm gelungen, nicht nachzugeben und seinen Überzeugungen als Jude treu zu bleiben, sogar als er die islamische intellektuelle Welt betrat, die ihn umgab. Der Maimonides, den Baeck hier darstellte, war ein Vorbild seines Zeitalters: ein Vorbild moralischer Integrität. Aber nicht nur für eine vergangene Zeit. Baeck beendete seinen Vortrag, gehalten für Deutsche auf deutschem Boden, mit den folgenden Worten: „Das war dieser Mann, Rabbi Moses ben Maimon, der Rambam. Seiner gedenken, heißt, an uns eine Frage richten, die uns selbst gilt."

Anders als manche deutsch-jüdischen Flüchtlinge und Überlebende weigerte sich Baeck, sich wieder in Deutschland niederzulassen. In einem Interview mit der amerikanisch-jüdischen Zeitung Aufbau sagte Baeck 1945:

Die Geschichte des deutschen Judentums ist definitiv zu Ende. Die Uhr kann nicht zurückgestellt werden. [...] Eine Rückkehr nach Deutschland? Ich sehe für Juden keinerlei Möglichkeit hierzu. Zwischen den deutschen Juden und dem Deutschland der Epoche 1933–45 steht zu viel. Soviel Mord, Raub und Plünderung, soviel Blut und Tränen und Gräber können nicht ausgelöscht werden. [...] Gewiss werden einzelne Gemeinden hier und da fortexistieren, doch die nährende Humusschicht ist nicht mehr vorhanden.

Baeck beschränkte die Verantwortlichkeit der Deutschen nicht auf einige Wenige. „Die gesamte Nation nahm aktiv an dem Verbrechen an den Juden teil, fand Gefallen daran und versuchte, sich daran zu bereichern", sagte er in einem anderen Interview. Gleichzeitig erkannte er jedoch Ausnahmefälle an. An Elly Heuss-Knapp, die Frau des ersten Deutschen Bundespräsidenten, schrieb er im Jahre 1951:

Wir sollten, wenn wir an die Jahre der Niedertracht denken, und denken müssen, doch nie vergessen, dass es [...] Menschen gegeben hat, [...] die ‚schlicht mit ihrem Gotte gingen,' und die nun Fürbitter für ihr Volk sein dürfen. Ich habe in den bösen und bösesten Tagen solche Menschen kennen gelernt, und es ist mir wie eine Lebensaufgabe, zu beweisen, dass ich ihnen innig dankbar bin.

Es gab deutsche Christen, denen ihr Glaube den Mut verliehen hatte, sich gegen die Nazis aufzulehnen, ebenso wie das Judentum Baeck Mut gegeben hatte. Auch sie hatten das „Du sollst!" vernommen. Was die Nachkriegsgeneration in Deutschland anbelangte, war Baeck nicht einer derjenigen, der ihr die Schuld für die Sünden ihrer Eltern gab. Außerdem erkannte er trotz seines anfänglichen Pessimismus bald die Notwendigkeit, sich mit den religiösen Bedürfnissen der neu auflebenden Jüdischen Gemeinde auseinanderzusetzen. Er korrespondierte mit seinen ehemaligen Studenten an der Hochschule, Peter Levinson und Raphael Robert Geis, die als Rabbiner in den neuen deutsch-jüdischen Gemeinden tätig waren, und stand ihnen mit Rat, wie sie am besten ihre rabbinischen Aufgaben erfüllen konnten, zur Seite.

Nach dieser Übersicht über die für mich besonders relevanten Aspekte in Baecks Leben, seinem religiösen Gedankengut und den Vorzügen seines Charakters möchte ich nun der Frage nachgehen, was Leo Baeck für das Progressive Judentum im 21. Jahrhundert bedeuten kann, im Besonderen, was Baeck uns, die wir uns hier 50 Jahre nach seinem Tod in der Stadt, in der er 20 Jahre lebte und fungierte, versammelt haben, sagen kann.

Zuerst sollten wir uns daran erinnern, dass Baeck weder ein klassischer Reformjude im Sinne des amerikanischen Reformjudentums von vor 100 Jahren, noch des deutschen Gegenstücks, der Berliner Reformgemeinde, war. Joachim Prinz berichtet, dass Baeck persönlich die Ritualgesetze des Judentums einhielt; Prinz ging sogar so soweit, Baecks Praxis orthodox zu nennen. Wäre das nicht der Fall gewesen, wäre es fragwürdig, ob er solch weitreichenden Respekt unter den traditionellen Juden genossen hätte. Als Baeck dann nach dem Krieg am Hebrew Union College in Cincinnati unterrichtete und im Studentenheim wohnte, erschien er, wie es in jenen Tagen üblich war, ohne Kopfbedeckung zu Gottesdiensten in der Synagoge des College. Während seines Studiums hebräischer Texte in seinem Zimmer jedoch, trug er seine Jarmulke, wie er es seit vielen Jahren immer getan hatte. Im Privaten fromm, jedoch in der Öffentlichkeit flexibel gegenüber Ritualen, war Baeck ohne Frage ein *kelal jisraelnik*. Er respektierte die Bräuche anderer Juden, sogar wenn diese seinen eigenen Praktiken widersprachen. Er selbst war ein Produkt sowohl der konservativen als auch der liberalen Rabbinerseminare, der auch Kurse an einer *jeschiva* in Berlin belegt hatte, und er glaubte, dass es wünschenswert sei, dass alle Rabbinerstudenten mit mehr als nur einem Zweig des Judentums in Berührung kamen.

Jakob Petuchowski, *zichrono livracha*, der wegen Baeck nach Cincinnati kam, um dort unter ihm zu studieren, erinnert daran, dass sein Lehrer oft vom „großen Judentum" sprach, womit er die Religion aller Juden meinte, im Gegensatz zu den „kleinen Judentümern", womit er die verschiedenen Strömungen des Judentums bezeichnete, die von Adjektiven wie reformiert, konservativ und orthodox definiert waren. Nach Petuchowski betonte Baeck immer, dass das Substantiv wichtiger als das Adjektiv sei. Er hätte den Splittertendenzen am Rande der Jüdischen Gemeinde, die auf ihre Unterschiede zu anderen Juden pochten, nicht wohlwollend gegenüber gestanden. Auf einer Konferenz der World Union for Progressive Judaism sagte Baeck im Jahre 1946 auf Englisch: „We are Progressive, Liberal Jews, not for the sake of Progressive, Liberal Judaism, but for the sake of Judaism, of Judaism as a whole." Sektierertum und Synkretismus mit dem Christentum sind auch weiterhin eine Bedrohung für das Progressive Judentum im 21. Jahrhundert. Auch wenn wir an unseren Prinzipien festhalten, akzeptierten wir Baecks Verständnis unserer Bewegung, sähen wir uns immer zuerst als Juden und erst dann als progressive Juden.

Es muss zugegeben werden, dass Leo Baeck sicherlich kein Feminist in dem Sinne war, dass er die Verwirklichung feministischer Prinzipien über seinen Wunsch, ein Maximum an Einheit innerhalb der Jüdischen Gemeinde zu bewahren, gesetzt hätte. Als in den letzten Jahren der Weimarer Republik die Synagoge in der Prinzregentenstraße hier in Berlin gebaut wurde und die Frage aufkam, ob Männer und Frauen zusammen sitzen sollten, zog Baeck eine Kompromisslösung vor, die Gemeindegliedern erlaubte, selbst zu entscheiden, ob sie in dem Teil der Synagoge mit gemischter oder in dem mit separater Sitzordnung sitzen wollten. Es war nicht Baeck, sondern Rabbi Max Dienemann, der das Diplom unterschrieb, das Regina Jonas zur ersten Rabbinerin machte. Baeck bezeugte jedoch am 6. Februar 1942 die korrekte Abschrift ihres hebräischen Rabbinatsdiploms, welches heute eingerahmt an einer Wand des Leo Baeck College in London hängt. Zumindest erkannte Baeck, dass ihre rabbinischen Tätigkeiten in jenen letzten schwierigen Monaten, bevor er und Rabbi Jonas nach Theresienstadt deportiert wurden, dringend willkommen geheißen wurden. Es ist schwer zu sagen, wie er heute jüdischem Feminismus gegenüberstehen würde – oder der kompletten religiösen Gleichstellung homosexueller Männer und Frauen. Ich sollte hoffen, dass er sie aufgrund seines Gerechtigkeitssinns zu schätzen wüsste. Ich denke aber auch, dass er uns in Bezug auf diese Fragen angemahnt hätte, unsere neuen Perspektiven im Zusammenhang mit der jüdischen Tradition zu sehen, die das Erbe aller Juden darstellt.

Baeck hätte sicherlich der Rede, die Rabbi Eric Yoffie auf der jüngsten Konferenz der Union for Reform Judaism in Houston, Texas hielt, zugestimmt, in der Rabbi Yoffie dazu aufrief, die Anstrengungen zu vermehren, Nicht-Juden zum Judentum zu bekehren. Baeck war selbst ein begeisterter Fürsprecher dafür, was man heute in Amerika „outreach" nennt. Nach dem Krieg, im Angesicht der Verluste durch den Holocaust, argumentierte er für eine aktive Kampagne der Konvertierung. 1950 schrieb er an einen Bekannten, dass jüdische Selbstachtung sie dringend erfordere:

> Eine Religion, die nicht nur existieren, sondern leben will, muss wie jeden wahren, echten Gedanken, so jedem wahrhaftigen echten Menschen erschlossen bleiben. Nur so kann sie auf die Dauer in der Gewissheit ihrer Wahrheit leben. Ein Glaube, der seine Tore verrammelte, würde innerlich verkümmern. Was keine Not vollbringen konnte und kann, würde er selber vollziehen, er würde im Angesicht der Menschen abdanken. Um das große Vertrauen, um die Bejahung unseres Judentums handelt es sich hier.

Wenn wir Baecks Botschaft für uns heute betrachten, sollten wir uns auch daran erinnern, dass er sich stetig aus der Sphäre von Hermann Cohens neo-Kant'schem Rationalismus heraus und auf eine Wertschätzung mystischer Erfahrungen zubewegte, die er wahrscheinlich aus Rudolf Ottos bahnbrechendem Buch „Das Heilige" zog. In einem seiner Briefe schreibt Baeck, dass er und seine Frau bei Otto in den späten 20er Jahren in Marburg zu Gast gewesen waren, als Baeck dort eine Vorlesungsreihe hielt, und das Paar „eine aufrichtige Zuneigung" für Otto empfunden hätte. In seinen eigenen Überlegungen fügte Baeck das Geheimnis dem Gebot als fundamentales Prinzip des Judentums hinzu. Auf zunehmende Weise sah er Gott nicht nur als einen gebietenden, sondern auch als einen liebenden Gott. Zu einer Zeit, in der der persönlichen religiösen Erfahrung und dem jüdischem Mystizismus wieder mehr Beachtung geschenkt werden, ist Baecks Balance des Moralischen und des Mystischen besonders ansprechend.

Leo Baeck war nicht uneingeschränkt religiöser Universalist. Sein letztes Hauptwerk „Dieses Volk: Jüdische Existenz" ist eine ausgeweitete Illustration von Gottes besonderer Beziehung zu seinem auserwählten Volk. Für Baeck war das Volk nicht weniger wichtig als die Lehre. Dennoch zeigen seine früheren und späteren Schriften, dass er das Judentum als eine universale Religion verstand, die jeglichen Chauvinismus verabscheute und den unkontrollierten Gebrauch von Macht ablehnte. Er identifizierte sich eher mit Propheten und Pharisäern als mit Königen und Priestern. Der zweite Teil der Bibel, die Propheten, so sagte er, könnte auch „die Propheten gegen den Staat" genannt werden. Obgleich er die Notwendigkeit staatlicher Macht anerkannte, bezeichnete er sie 1953 als „letzten Ausweg", der nur eingeschlagen werden sollte, wenn Überzeugungskraft versagte. Es war also keine Überraschung, dass er das Jewish Peace Fellowship unterstützte. Anders als die lutherische Religion, der Baeck so kritisch gegenüber stand, ist Baecks Judentum kein Glaube, der sich vom Staat abwendet. Er ist aber auch kein Glaube, der dem Staat Vorschriften macht, so wie es heutzutage der fundamentalistische Islam im Mittleren Osten, die evangelikalen Christen in den Vereinigten Staaten oder das orthodoxe Judentum in Israel tun. Für Baeck nimmt eine wahre Religion weder den einen noch den anderen Platz ein. Ihre Aufgabe gegenüber dem Staat ist, ihren moralischen Einfluss zu nutzen, um den Staat dem Königreich Gottes näher zu bringen, dem Königreich universaler Gleichberechtigung. Es liegt in der Natur des Staates, Kompromisse schließen zu müssen. Eine Religion jedoch sollte nie kompromissbereit sein. Daher kann sich Religion niemals mit dem Status Quo zufrieden geben. Baeck führte dies im Jahre 1953 so aus: „We believe in God and not in progress made. We therefore believe in the constant task, and not in the achievements." Das eine und universale Gebot Gottes kann niemals ganz erfüllt werden, aber seine partielle Erfüllung, so klein sie auch sein mag, ist deswegen kaum unwichtig. In einem seiner für mich bedeutungsvollsten Sätze schrieb Baeck: „Im Ringen um das nie endende, nie ganz erfüllte Gebot ‚heiligt sich' der

Mensch, oder wie dafür auch gesagt werden kann, gestaltet sich die Individualität des Menschen zur sittlichen Persönlichkeit."

Für Baeck repräsentiert der Staat Israel für die Juden, die dort leben, eine neue Prüfung der Botschaft des Judentums. Obwohl er es nie ausdrücklich sagte, muss er doch gehofft haben, dass in dem neuen Staat religiöse Führungskräfte geboren würden, die, wie die Propheten, den Staat für sein Handeln zur Rechenschaft ziehen und ihn an ihrem moralischen Ideal messen würden. Er hätte ein priesterliches Judentum in Israel, das der Staat unterstützt und das dem Staat seine beschränkten Interessen aufzwingt, während es das materielle Wohlergehen einer jeden Person, ob Jude oder Nicht-Jude, vernachlässigt, nicht gutheißen können. Baecks Botschaft der moralischen Verantwortung ist für den Staat Israel ebenso bedeutsam wie für die Diaspora.

Mein Interesse an Baeck im Jahre 2006 konzentriert sich jedoch noch immer auf die Worte, die sich in seinem klassischen Werk „Das Wesen des Judentums" finden: „Ich bin der Ewige, dein Gott, du sollst." Obwohl der Satz „Ich bin der Ewige, dein Gott" in der Tora oft vorkommt und ihm spezifische Gebote, von denen einige von menschlichen oder politischen Beziehungen, andere von Ritualen handeln, entweder folgen oder voranstehen, wählt Baeck nicht eines davon aus. Nicht einmal, um die Buber-Rosenzweig Übersetzung zu benutzen, den berühmten Satz: „Halte lieb deinen Genossen, dir gleich. Ich bin's." Und auch nicht die Zehn Gebote. Insofern als er dem Gebot Inhalt verleiht, geschieht das nur auf sehr allgemeine und undifferenzierte Art: „Ihr sollt heilig werden, denn heilig bin Ich euer Gott." Tatsächlich hat sich Baeck, indem er schreibt: „Ich bin der Ewige dein Gott, du sollst." am Hebräischen vergriffen, da es für „du sollst" ohne folgendes Verbum keine Entsprechung gibt. Was Baeck uns sagen will, ist, dass das Ewige und Göttliche keine spezifischen Gebote sind – diese müssen wir für uns selbst herausfinden – sondern das Bewusstsein, dass man gefordert wird. Und dieses Gefordertwerden lag für Baeck, so glaube ich, gänzlich auf dem Gebiet der Moral. Obwohl, wie schon erwähnt, er persönlich religiöse Rituale ausübte, glaubte Baeck nicht, dass diese von Gott geboten seien. Hier konvergiert seine Auffassung mit einem Prinzip, das die Reformbewegung von Anfang an charakterisiert hat: Rituale sind Mittel zu religiösem und moralischem Zweck, aber kein Zweck an sich.

Baeck stand der Religiosität sehr kritisch gegenüber, die wir ichbezogen nennen mögen. Ich glaube, er würde die heute übliche Konzentration auf Spiritualität, die das Leben in der Welt außer Acht lässt, scharf ablehnen. Er hätte vielleicht sogar gesagt, dass das Konzept der „romantischen Religion", die er im Paulinischen und Lutherischen Christentum verurteilte, sich in einige Strömungen des heutigen Judentums eingeschlichen hätte. Zu seiner Zeit unterschied er zwischen einer Religion, die sich auf religiöses Erleben stützte und einer die sich auf das Leben selbst gründete. Die erstere bezeichnete er als „religiösen Egotismus", weil sie sich auf die eigene Person, nicht auf die Ansprüche der Menschen an einander, konzentrierte. Wie bereits erwähnt, war Baeck ein Anhänger Kants und hielt daher Kants berühmten Satz, in dem der Königsberger Philosoph von zwei Quellen des Wunders sprach, in hohen Ehren: der gestirnte Himmel über uns und das moralische Gesetz in uns. Ich bin aber der Ansicht, dass es zum Verständnis Baecks unerlässlich ist, darauf hinzuweisen, dass er diese zwei Quellen religiöser Inspiration einer Rangordnung unterzog. Baeck schrieb:

In der Erfüllung des Gebotes wird eine Erhabenheit gefunden, die höher ist als die der beseelten Sternenwelt. Oder mit anderen Worten: Das moralische Gesetz in uns ist hier mehr noch als der gestirnte Himmel über uns.

Das Geheimnis ist sicherlich wichtig für Baeck, aber Geheimnis ohne Gebot entspricht nicht dem Judentum. Heiligung wird aus moralischem Handeln geboren.

Wir leben in einer Zeit, die sich nach Geheimnis sehnt, und oft vor Imperativen zurückscheut, die die Überwindung von Eigennutz erfordern, um das zu erreichen, was recht ist. Wir tun das „Angemessene" und vermeiden das „Unangemessene", aber uns fehlt oft das Bewusstsein eines Absoluten, das uns zwingt, moralische Kompromisse abzulehnen. Andererseits versuchen die, die ein Gefühl des Absoluten besitzen, oft, anderen ihren Willen aufzudrängen, anstatt erst mit sich selbst hart ins Gericht zu gehen. Wir nennen die, die Politik oder sogar Gewalt benutzen, um anderen ihre religiösen Absolute aufzuzwingen, zu Recht „Fanatiker". Und sie stellen kein geringeres moralisches Problem dar als die Relativisten. Es war Baecks Verantwortungsgefühl gegenüber einem höheren Willen zusammen mit einem bestimmten Ausmaß an Toleranz gegenüber den Ansichten anderer, die ihm die Kraft verliehen, in dem Morast Nazi-Deutschlands nicht nur physisch, sondern auch moralisch zu überleben. Unsere Zeiten sind, trotz aller moralischen Kompromisse, zu denen sie öffentliche und private Persönlichkeiten verleiten, glücklicherweise ganz anders als das Deutschland von vor 70 Jahren. Aber auch sie verlangen, dass wir uns immer wieder entscheiden, ob wir uns fügen und Kompromisse eingehen, oder ob wir uns ein Pflichtgefühl bewahren wollen, dessen Ursprünge wir mit Gott verbinden.

Für Baeck lag das Wesen des wahren Progressiven Judentums nicht in einer Bewegung der religiösen, geschweige denn der moralischen Anpassung. Seine Aufgabe, so erklärte er in einer Ansprache auf der World Union-Konferenz 1928 hier in Berlin, war nicht, den Zeitgeist zu imitieren. „Eine zeitgemäße Religion, ein zeitgemäßes Judentum," sagte er damals, „das wäre ein Widerspruch in sich, eine contradictio in adjecto […]. Die Juden sind immer die Unzeitgemäßen."

Die Aufgabe des Judentums, wie Baeck sie verstand, ist es, solange in Opposition zu stehen, bis das Königreich Gottes auf Erden errichtet ist. Dies war Baecks Messianismus: moralisch verankert zu sein in dem messianischen Zeitalter, von dem die Propheten träumten. Lassen Sie mich also mit einem Paradox abschließen: Baecks Vermächtnis für das heutige Progressive Judentum ist, dass es kein zeitgemäßes, kein Judentum von heute sein soll, sondern ein Judentum, das eine noch unerreichte moralische Zukunft anstrebt. Indem er darauf beharrte, sein Leben so gut und so mutig wie möglich zu leben, im Einklang mit der transzendenten göttlichen Quelle des moralischen Gebots und der Zukunft, auf die sie hinzeigt, kann Baeck, sogar 50 Jahre nach seinem Tod, auch weiterhin als unser Mentor dienen.

Esther Seidel

Leo Baecks Stimme des Ausgleichs im Konflikt zwischen liberalem Judentum und liberalem Protestantismus[1]

Der Konflikt, von dem hier die Rede ist, fand zu Beginn des 20. Jahrhunderts zwischen protestantischen Theologieprofessoren und jüdischen Gelehrten statt und hatte eine Vorgeschichte. Obwohl die deutschen Juden zwar endlich seit etwa 30 Jahren gleichberechtigte Bürger im vereinten Deutschland waren, musste sich die kulturelle und vor allem die religiöse Geltung des Judentums wiederholt in Auseinandersetzung mit den Überlegenheitsansprüchen des liberalen Protestantismus behaupten.[2] Hierbei ging es für die jüdische Religion um nichts weniger als um ihre Existenzberechtigung gegen eine „wachsende Erbitterung der Protestanten über den festen Willen des Judentums zur Bewahrung seiner besonderen Identität".[3] Als noch 1910 der Berliner Rechtshistoriker Josef Kohler den Übertritt der Juden zum Protestantismus als Bedingung für eine vollständige Assimilation der Juden in die deutsche Gesellschaft forderte, wies Leo Baeck dies zurück: es gäbe sehr wohl wesentliche Gegensätze zwischen Judentum und Protestantismus, und der Wert einer Minorität bestünde gerade auch in ihrem Willen zur Individualität. In einer modernen Kultur dürfe keine Religion einen Absolutheitsanspruch stellen.[4]

Charakteristisch war es für Leo Baeck, an diese Zurückweisung der protestantischen Forderung gleich auch eine Verpflichtung für das Judentum anzuknüpfen, nämlich „das eigene jüdische Selbstverständnis darzulegen und deutlich zu betonen".[5] Die Grundlagen dazu hatte er selber in seinem Buch „Das Wesen des Judentums" (1905) aufgezeigt, einem Werk, das nach den Worten des protestantischen Theologen Christian Wiese gelten darf als eine „glänzende Apologie des

---

[1] Vortrag gehalten im Domforum zu Köln am 2. März 2006 auf Einladung des katholischen Bildungswerkes.

[2] Vgl. Christian Wiese. *Ein unerhörtes Gesprächsangebot. Leo Baeck, die Wissenschaft des Judentums und das Judentumsbild des liberalen Protestantismus.* In: *Leo Baeck 1873–1956. Aus dem Stamme von Rabbinern.* Georg Heuberger und Fritz Backhaus (Hrsg.). Frankfurt/Main: Jüdischer Verlag, 2001, S. 147–171, hier S. 156.

[3] Ibd., S. 158.

[4] Vgl. ibd., S. 153.

[5] Ibd., S. 160.

Judentums als der ethischen Vernunftreligion par excellence, die mehr als nur Gleichwertigkeit mit dem Christentum beanspruchen konnte".[6]

Dieses Buch Baecks war zunächst die Antwort auf Adolf von Harnack, bzw. auf dessen 1899 in Berlin vor 600 Studenten aller Fakultäten gehaltene Vorlesungsreihe, die dann als Buch mit dem Titel „Das Wesen des Christentums" erschien.

Professor von Harnack war nicht nur der berühmteste Kirchenhistoriker und die protestantische Autorität seiner Zeit; er war auch Präsident der Preußischen Akademie der Wissenschaften und Berater des Kaisers. Harnack, der persönlich nicht anti-jüdisch eingestellt war, stellte ein Christentum vor, das allein aus der „Kraft des Evangeliums Jesu" heraus verstanden werden sollte. Seine Vorgehensweise und antijüdischen Werturteile gaben dabei in jüdischen Kreisen Anlass zu größter Besorgnis und forderten auch eine wissenschaftliche Kritik seiner Methode heraus. Hauptexponent dieser Kritik war der junge Leo Baeck.

Nach einer Lebensskizze von Leo Baeck sollen einige wenige Textproben aus Harnacks Werk in den Zusammenhang seiner liberal-protestantischen Absicht gestellt werden. Folgen werden dann bestimmte Kritikpunkte aus der Sicht Baecks wie auch eine Analyse seiner „Auseinandersetzung" mit Harnacks Ideen durch kritische Stimmen in der gegenwärtigen protestantischen Theologie. Daran schließen sich Grundideen Baecks hinsichtlich seines Entwurfs zu einem liberalen Judentum an, wobei Passagen einfließen werden aus einem Vortrag, den Leo Baeck in den fünfziger Jahren in London vornehmlich vor deutsch-jüdischen Flüchtlingen auf Deutsch gehalten hat.[7]

Leo Baeck wurde 1873 in Lissa in der Provinz Posen geboren und entstammte durch beide Eltern einer Reihe von Rabbinern. Sein Vater, Rabbiner Samuel Bäck, hatte in Leipzig promoviert, und Baeck wuchs als einer unter elf Geschwistern auf in einer Atmosphäre von jüdischer und weltlicher Gelehrsamkeit und Offenheit. Die Juden des Großherzogtum Posens, ganze 6% der Bevölkerung,[8] fühlten sich

---

[6] Christian Wiese. *Wissenschaft des Judentums und protestantische Theologie im wilhelminischen Deutschland. Ein Schrei ins Leere.* Schriftenreihe wissenschaftlicher Abhandlungen des Leo-Baeck-Instituts, 61. Tübingen: Mohr Siebeck, 1999, S. 135.

[7] Dieser Vortrag „Individualität im Judentum", den Leo Baeck in den 50er Jahren in London gehalten hat, liegt als undatierte Kassettenaufnahme in der Bibliothek des Leo Baeck College, London vor.

[8] Als größte Tuchmacherstadt in Großpolen mit überwiegend jüdischem Anteil im Tuchhandel konnte Lissa auch die größte jüdische Gemeinde vorweisen, die jedoch seit der preußischen Übernahme 1793 durch Abwanderung der Juden in den erhofften wirtschaftlich reicheren und menschenrechtlich aufgeklärteren Westen Preußens von fast 5000 Einwohnern im Jahre 1765 auf nur noch 1206 im Jahre 1895 herabsank. Vgl. hierzu: Susanne Plietzsch. *Kindheit und Jugend Leo Baecks in Lissa.* In: *Leo Baeck 1873–1956. Aus dem Stamme von Rabbinern.* Georg Heuberger und Fritz Backhaus (Hrsg.). Frankfurt/Main: Jüdischer Verlag, 2001, S. 15–25.

preußisch und lebten in Eintracht mit den Protestanten, Katholiken und Calvinisten, ein Umstand, der Baecks liberale Haltung geprägt haben mag. Von besonderem Einfluss auf sein Leben war nach seinen eigenen Worten seine Gymnasialzeit am Comenius Gymnasium, an dem er in Latein, Griechisch und Mathematik hervorragende Noten erzielte. Was er dort gelernt hatte, blieb zeitlebens seinem Gedächtnis verhaftet, und dieser geistige Besitz half, ihm selbst und vielen anderen während seiner Internierung im KZ Theresienstadt Trost zu spenden.

1891 begann Leo Baeck seine Rabbinerausbildung am konservativen Breslauer Rabbinerseminar und studierte gleichzeitig an der Breslauer Universität Philosophie im Hauptfach. Zwei Jahre später wechselte er nach Berlin über, wo er bei Wilhelm Dilthey mit einer Dissertation über „Spinozas erste Einwirkungen in Deutschland" promovierte und daneben an der dortigen liberalen Hochschule für die Wissenschaft des Judentums seine rabbinischen Studien fortsetzte. Seine bewusst angestrebte Kenntnis der verschiedenen jüdischen Strömungen von liberal bis orthodox prädestinierten ihn später dazu, die Führung des deutschen Judentums zu übernehmen.

Als junger Rabbiner wirkte er zuerst in Oppeln, dann ab 1907 in Düsseldorf, wo er die Bat Mitzwa für die Mädchen einführte. Ab 1912 lehrte er in Berlin an seiner alten Rabbinerausbildungsstätte, der Hochschule für die Wissenschaft des Judentums, Midrasch und Homiletik. Während des ersten Weltkrieges war Baeck als Feldrabbiner in Frankreich und Litauen tätig und verfasste ein Feldgebetbuch für die jüdischen Soldaten. Laut Baecks späterer Biographen zeigte er bereits in der Kriegszeit tiefen sittlichen Ernst, hohes Verantwortungsbewusstsein und ausgeprägtes Pflichtgefühl.

1933 wurde Baeck zum Präsidenten der Reichsvertretung der deutschen Juden gewählt, weil „in einer solchen Zeit der Not ein Mann erforderlich" war, der „mit dem Rüstzeug, das unsere Propheten besaßen", ausgestattet war und „der aus seinem lebendigen Gottesglauben und der Liebe zum jüdischen Volke die tiefsten Kräfte zog".[9] Es war eine zwiespältige, nahezu ohnmächtige Position, die zunächst Hilfe bei der Auswanderung der deutschen Juden,[10] dann deren Ausbildung, Dokumenten- und Geldtransfers umfasste, schließlich aber nur noch „im Verlangsamen des Unvermeidlichen", im „Kampf um Aufschub" zwischen sofor-

---

[9] Albert Friedlander. *Leo Baeck – Leben und Lehre*. Stuttgart: Deutsche Verlagsanstalt, 1973, S. 52. Friedlander zitiert Bruno Italiener nach Eva G. Reichmann. *Festschrift zum 80. Geburtstag von Rabbiner Dr. Leo Baeck am 23. Mai 1953*. London: Council for the Protection of the Rights and Interests of Jews from Germany, 1953, S. 41–42.

[10] Das System der jüdischen Selbsthilfe rettete mehr als die Hälfte der 1933 in Deutschland lebenden Juden.

tigem Tod und baldigem Tod bestehen konnte.[11] Baeck bemerkte, dass die tausendjährige Geschichte des deutschen Judentums an ihr Ende gekommen war und beschloss, trotz mancher Einladung ins Ausland, so lange selbst noch auf deutschem Boden zu bleiben, bis auch der letzte Jude Deutschland verlassen haben würde.

Im Januar 1943 wurde Leo Baeck, siebzigjährig, in das KZ Theresienstadt deportiert, nachdem er 50 Reichsmark für den Transport zu zahlen hatte. In Theresienstadt lebten damals 45.000 Menschen, vornehmlich alte und gebrechliche, auf engstem Raum. In den letzten dreieinhalb Jahren des Nationalsozialismus wurden noch 141.000 Menschen nach Theresienstadt deportiert und 88.000 davon weiter nach Osten, vor allem nach Auschwitz. In Theresienstadt starben 33.000 Menschen, während 23.000 in diesem Vorzeigelager der Nazi Propaganda überlebten, dass das Internationale Rote Kreuz und damit auch die übrige Welt über das Massenvernichtungsprogramm hinwegtäuschen sollte.[12] Insgesamt wurden circa 118.000 der nach Theresienstadt deportierten Menschen um ihr Leben gebracht.

Aus jener Zeit werden folgende Tätigkeiten Leo Baecks im KZ dokumentiert: zunächst sein Erlernen der tschechischen Sprache, aber auch die ihm zugeteilte Abfallbeseitigung, dann Krankenpflege und -seelsorge neben den nur aus seinem Gedächtnis gehaltenen philosophischen und theologischen Vorträgen über Platon, Spinoza, Kant, Maimonides usw., die von Hunderten besucht wurden. In dieser „Akademie des Überlebens" hielten 516 Referenten, darunter die erste Rabbinerin der Welt, die Deutsche Regina Jonas,[13] die mit ihrer Mutter hierher transportiert worden war, zwischen Sept. 1942 und Sept. 1944 circa 2280 Vorträge,[14] von denen die meisten die fehlende Schulbildung der Kinder ersetzen sollten und zudem für alle als „geistiger Widerstand" gedacht waren, der das Überleben ermöglichen sollte. Während jener Zeit im KZ schrieb Leo Baeck auch an einem Buch mit dem Titel „Dieses Volk", wann immer sich ein leeres Blatt fand.

Nach der Befreiung des Lagers durch sowjetische Truppen betreute Baeck noch die Typhuskranken, bevor er nach London geflogen wurde. Nur sehr selten sprach er danach über seine Erfahrungen in jener Zeit. Er hatte im Lager drei Viertel seiner eigenen Familie verloren: vier Schwestern und zwei Brüder, und etliche Freunde und Kollegen.

---

[11] Friedlander, S. 53.

[12] Vgl. Fritz Backhaus. *Ein Experiment des Willens zum Bösen. Überleben in Theresienstadt.* In: *Leo Baeck 1873–1956. Aus dem Stamme von Rabbinern.* In: Georg Heuberger und Fritz Backhaus (Hrsg.). Frankfurt/Main: Jüdischer Verlag, 2001, S. 111–128, hier S. 112.

[13] Leo Baeck hatte noch ihre Ordination befürwortet.

[14] Vgl. ibd., S. 119.

Die letzten Lebensjahre verbrachte Baeck in London, wo seine Tochter Ruth lebte. Er folgte noch im hohen Alter Einladungen an das Hebrew Union College in Cincinnati und besuchte auch Israel. Bereits 1948 verbrachte er sieben Wochen in Deutschland, hielt Vorlesungen in überfüllten Hörsälen, sprach im Düsseldorfer Landtag über Maimonides und traf den Bundespräsidenten Theodor Heuss in freundschaftlicher Verbundenheit.

1955 wurde das Leo Baeck Institut zur Erforschung der Geschichte der deutschen Juden in London gegründet und ein Jahr später das Leo Baeck College als Rabbinerausbildungsstätte. Leo Baeck begrüßte diese Einrichtung noch, bevor er im selben Jahr, 1956, verschied.

Wenden wir uns nun Adolf von Harnack zu, dessen Vorlesungen nach 100 Jahren gerade wieder neu verlegt worden sind. Gelten sie nur einem historischen Interesse oder reflektieren sie einen auch noch heute vertretenen Standpunkt?

Harnack gab vor, durch eine rein historische Verfahrensweise die treue Botschaft Jesu darstellen zu wollen. Wenn sich das dem Christentum Wesentliche erst, wie Harnack behauptet, entwicklungsgeschichtlich zeigt,[15] wie kann er kurz danach von einem ewig gültigen Evangelium außerhalb der Zeit sprechen? Harnack unterscheidet das Evangelium Jesu von den bekannten vier Evangelien, wobei er zugesteht, dass das von Johannes ein Sonderfall mit viel „Erdachtem" sei. Die Evangelien seien einerseits keine Geschichtswerke,[16] weil sie für die Evangelisation geschrieben wurden,[17] andererseits aber seien sie als Geschichtsquellen „nicht unbrauchbar". Mit welchen Kriterien Harnack Fiktion und Geschichte auseinander halten will, sagt er uns nicht.

Harnack räumt ein, dass wir über Jesu Leben so gut wie nichts wissen,[18] und misst der Geburtsgeschichte Jesu fast keine Bedeutung bei, um zwei Sätze weiter zu behaupten: „Aus dem Schweigen über die 30 ersten Jahre Jesu und aus dem, was die Evangelien von der Zeit seiner Berufswirksamkeit nicht berichten, lässt sich Wichtiges lernen."[19] Dies scheint absurd, denn wo man aus Schweigen lernt, sprechen wir von Mystik, nicht aber von Wissenschaft. Harnack war ja als Präsident der Preußischen Akademie der Wissenschaften Repräsentant der deutschen Wissenschaften schlechthin. Höflich, aber bestimmt, hat dann auch Baecks

---

[15] Vgl. Adolf von Harnack. *Das Wesen des Christentums. Sechzehn Vorlesungen vor Studierenden aller Fakultäten im Wintersemester 1899/1900 an der Universität Berlin gehalten von Adolf v. Harnack*. Claus-Dieter Osthövener (Hrsg.). Tübingen: Mohr Siebeck, 2005, S. 15f (Erstmalig ersch. in Leipzig: Hinrichs, 1900).
[16] Ibd. S. 20.
[17] Ibd. S. 21.
[18] Ibd. S. 26.
[19] Ibd. S. 28.

Rezension des Harnackschen Werkes, die 1901 erschien, in den Worten des bedeutenden protestantischen Theologen Friedrich-Wilhelm Marquard, jeden möglichen Respekt vor Harnacks Wissenschaft unterminiert.[20]

Weitere Widersprüchlichkeiten treten bei der Zentralfigur, Jesus selber, auf. Was bedeutet es, wenn Harnack behauptet, dass aus Jesus alles „klar und ungehemmt" hervorströme,[21] er es jedoch nicht zeige, um gleich darauf von Jesu Rede zu behaupten, sie zeige „die ganze Stufenleiter der Affekte, [...] Töne leidenschaftlicher Anklage [...], [und dann] eine stille, gleichmäßige Sammlung [...] ein Beweis intensiver Ruhe".[22] Hier häufen sich die Widersprüche, wie auch in den folgenden Sätzen:

Zum Predigtstil Jesu sagt Harnack: „Er hat wie ein Prophet gesprochen und doch nicht wie ein Prophet. Friede [...] atmen seine Worte. Er drängt auf Kampf [...] alles in dem ruhigen Gleichmaß der Gleichnisse."[23]

„Und was hat nun Jesus an Neuem gebracht?" Harnack stellt und beantwortet die Frage selbst: „Meine Herren! Die Frage nach dem Neuen in der Religion ist keine Frage, die von solchen gestellt wird, die in ihr leben."[24] Harnack spricht dann weiter von einer „Umwertung aller Werte" und legt Jesus folgende Parolen als Essenzen des Christentums in den Mund: „Nur wer sein Leben verliert, wird es gewinnen" und „nur wer seine Seele haßt, wird sie bewahren."[25]

Kein Jude würde sich in diesen Sätzen wieder finden bzw. ihnen zustimmen, und daher ist zu vermuten, dass der Jude Jesus sie so nicht geäußert haben wird. Und dann folgt endlich ein Satz, dem ein logisch Denkender aus ganzem Herzen zustimmen kann: „Wir müssen uns klar machen, wie paradox dies alles ist, ja, dass die Paradoxie der Religion erst hier zu ihrem vollen Ausdruck kommt."[26]

Leo Baeck hat deshalb später das Christentum als eine „romantische" Religion bezeichnet, weil es stark durch das Irrationale gekennzeichnet sei. Wie sah seine Antwort auf Harnack aus?

Vor allem wendet sich Baeck gegen Harnacks Versuch, Jesus und das überhaupt erst in der Entstehung begriffene Christentum von seinen jüdisch-historischen Wurzeln abzukoppeln. Harnack hatte der jüdischen Überlieferung zwar

---

[20] Vgl. Friedrich-Wilhelm Marquard. *Unabgegoltenes in der Kritik Leo Baecks an Adolf Harnack*. In: *Leo Baeck – Lehrer und Helfer in schwerer Zeit*. Werner Licharz (Hrsg.). Arnoldshainer Texte, 20. Frankfurt/Main: Haag & Herchen, 1983, S. 173.
[21] Vgl. Harnack, S. 28.
[22] Ibd. S. 29.
[23] Ibd. S. 30.
[24] Ibd. S. 34.
[25] Ibd. S. 46.
[26] Ibd. S. 46.

eine „reiche und tiefe Ethik" zugestanden,[27] doch wurde dieser Lehrinhalt dann bei den Pharisäern „beschwert, getrübt, verzerrt, unwirksam gemacht, um seinen Ernst gebracht [...] verunreinigt".[28] Wie sollte dies gekommen sein? Harnack hat die Antwort: Moral wurde unter pharisäischer Anleitung in ihr Gegenteil verwandelt durch die „Verflechtung mit dem Kultus und die Versteinerung im Ritual".[29] Darauf musste Baeck unbedingt antworten.

Gestatten Sie mir, an dieser Stelle Harnacks Absicht kurz zusammenzufassen: Es gibt für Harnack keinen Fortschritt zum Königreich Gottes ohne die Predigt Jesu, und seine theologische Position zwang ihn dazu, Jesu Evangelium als etwas Einzigartiges zu betonen. Deshalb durfte keinerlei Abhängigkeit von zeitgenössischem Dasein den Charakter der „Zeitlosigkeit" und „ideellen Reinheit" der Botschaft Jesu verderben, auf den Harnack den Anspruch absoluter Wahrheit gründen wollte,[30] und deshalb musste er „den Abstand zwischen Jesus und seiner jüdischen Umwelt aufs schärfste [herausarbeiten]. Demgegenüber besteht Baeck auf der These, dass ein wahres Verständnis Jesu unmöglich sei, wenn man seine Gestalt aus ihrer intimen Verbindung mit der Frömmigkeit seines Volkes löst."[31] Christian Wiese führt weiterhin aus christlicher Sicht aus, dass der Begriff des Wesens – denn es ging ja um das Wesen des Christentums – auf das Wertvolle und Bleibende abzielte, welches nach Harnacks Überzeugung in der ursprünglichen Verkündigung Jesu als vollkommene Gotteserkenntnis beschlossen läge. Gemessen an Jesu gelebter Botschaft erschien Harnack die spätere christliche dogmengeschichtliche Entwicklung nur als eine „Schale" des Christentums, die zwar ihr historisches Recht besaß, aber nicht den eigentlichen „Kern" ausmachte.[32] Während das Judentum zu Jesu Zeiten nach Harnack im Ritualismus erstarrt war und seine Berechtigung verloren hatte, überwand Jesus das ganze festgefahrene und unflexible Judentum durch einen völligen Neubeginn, bis dann Paulus mit seiner Interpretation Christi als Auflösung und Ende des Gesetzes den radikalen Bruch vollzog.[33]

Gegen diese Herauslösung Jesu aus seinem jüdischen Hintergrund wendet sich Baeck ganz entschieden und wirft Harnack Ungeschichtlichkeit und Ungerech-

---

[27] Ibd. S. 47.
[28] Ibd. S. 35.
[29] Ibd. S. 47.
[30] Vgl. Hans Liebeschütz. *Leo Baeck. Judentum und Protestantismus*. In: *Von Georg Simmel zu Franz Rosenzweig*. Hans Liebeschütz (Hrsg.). Schriftenreihe wissenschaftlicher Abhandlungen des Leo-Baeck-Instituts, 23. Tübingen: Mohr, 1970, S. 55–102, hier S. 58.
[31] Ibd. S. 59.
[32] Vgl. Wiese, *Wissenschaft des Judentums*, S. 133.
[33] Vgl. ibd., S. 134.

tigkeit vor, d.h. eine Herabsetzung der hebräischen Bibel, das Verschweigen der Fortexistenz eines lebendigen Judentums nebst einem völligen Ignorieren seines Selbstverständnisses, die Präsentation eines Zerrbildes des Pharisäertums, eine völlige Unkenntnis jüdischer Quellen und eine Nichtwahrnehmung der Arbeiten jüdischer Forscher zum Thema.[34]

Ein Historiker dürfe nicht sein eigenes, späteres Urteil der dargestellten Zeit überstülpen, nicht seine Wertkategorien zu denen jener fernen Vergangenheit machen. Nicht die Vergangenheit werde hier vor uns hingestellt, sondern die Projektion eines vorher bzw. eher nachher! gefassten Bildes in die Vergangenheit hinein.[35]

Um Jesu und seine Zeit zu verstehen, müsse man eher in hebräischen und aramäischen Begriffen denken, die leider allzu oft fehlerhaft bzw. tendenziös ins Griechische, Lateinische, Deutsche übertragen und dann mit nachträglicher christlicher Bedeutung überlagert worden seien. Das messianische Zeitalter sei für das Judentum etwas anderes als das christliche Reich Gottes, die jüdische Tora sei nicht deckungsgleich mit dem christlichen Offenbarungsbegriff, unsere Gottesbegriffe seien nicht identisch, und wir sprächen selten die gleiche Sprache, wenn es um religiöse Begriffe geht.

Gegen Harnacks These, Jesus habe die Verbindung zum Gesetz gelöst und sei auf die Gesinnung und Liebe zurückgegangen,[36] zeigt Baeck auf, wie das Gebot der Nächstenliebe im Judentum vor allem durch die großen Gesetzeslehrer Hillel, einen Zeitgenossen Jesu, und Akiba auf den Punkt gebracht worden war, nachdem schon in Lev 19,18 steht: וְאָהַבְתָּ לְרֵעֲךָ כָּמוֹךָ – *we-ahavta le-re'echa kamocha* – „Du sollst deinen Nächsten lieben, denn er ist wie du." Die Kirchengeschichte hatte es vermieden, im Judentum zu unterscheiden zwischen dem ethisch-sittlichen Postulat und den ritualgesetzlichen Entscheidungen, so dass Harnack zu der absurden These kam, Jesus habe mit scharfem Schnitt die Verbindung der Ethik mit dem äußeren Kultus gelöst.[37] „Die Ethik", lenkt Baeck ein, „war jedoch ganz und gar nicht mit dem Kultus […] verknüpft, sondern vollkommen unabhängig von ihm".[38]

Die Rolle des Kultus oder der Halacha sei es, nur auf sittliche Zwecke hinzuleiten, aber diese Rituale seien keinesfalls so bedeutsam wie die Gebote der Ethik.

---

[34] Vgl. ibd., S. 136f.
[35] Vgl. Leo Baecks Rezension zu *Harnack's Vorlesungen über das Wesen des Christenthums*. In: MGWJ, 1901, Heft 2, S. 97–120. Auch abgedruckt in: *Leo Baeck – Lehrer und Helfer in schwerer Zeit*. Werner Licharz (Hrsg.). Arnoldshainer Texte, 20. Frankfurt/Main: Haag & Herchen, 1983, S. 11–34, hier S. 13f.
[36] Harnack, S. 47.
[37] Ibd., S. 45.
[38] Baeck, *Harnack's Vorlesungen*, S. 28.

Am Versöhnungstag erbitten die Juden nur um Vergebung derjenigen Sünden, die allein ethisches Fehlverhalten betreffen, nicht aber um Vergebung für Verstöße gegen das Ritual.

Marquard schreibt diese fälschliche christliche Identifizierung von jüdischem Gesetz und jüdischer Religion der Unfähigkeit zu, Haggada und Halacha nicht zu unterscheiden und aufeinander beziehen zu können. In Anspielung auf die Lehre Luthers von der erlösenden Gnade, der der Mensch nur Glauben, aber kein Tun entgegenbringen kann, schreibt Marquard selbstkritisch:

> Da wir Christen, zumal wir protestantischen, das Tun so hoch [wie die Juden] unmöglich schätzen wollen, schieben wir den Juden das [rituelle] Tun als ihre einzige Religion zu. Welcher Unsinn![39]

Die Tora sei jedoch Geschichtserzählung, Exegese und Gesetz in einem, alles untrennbar miteinander verwoben, und die Bedeutung dieses Phänomens sei von der christlichen Theologie nicht reflektiert worden.

Baeck tritt auch dem christlichen Vorwurf der damaligen Unterdrückung der Armen entgegen, hätten doch gerade die Pharisäer die Armen unter Rechtsschutz und Fürsorge gestellt.[40]

Der Begriff „Pharisäer" wurde im christlichen Verständnis durch die Evangelien zum Schimpfwort. Die Evangelien sind, Generationen nach Jesu Tod verfasst, ein Produkt der Abgrenzung zum Judentum und konstruierten deshalb Jesu Feindlichkeit gegenüber den Pharisäern. Der Name „Pharisäer" leitet sich von hebräisch *peruschim*, „die sich Absondernden" her. Der Name war ein Spitzname, der den Pharisäern von den rivalisierenden Sadduzäern gegeben worden war, weil die Pharisäer, die sich selber *chachamim*, Gelehrte, nannten, das mündliche Gesetz bis auf den Punkt befolgten und sich aus Gründen der rituellen Reinheit absonderten. Darüber hinaus war es ihr Ziel, das Judentum von einer Tempelreligion mit erblicher Priesterschaft – das waren die Sadduzäer – in eine Volksreligion zu verwandeln, und um das zu erreichen, traten sie für eine neue Form von demokratischem Gottesdienst in den Synagogen ein, ohne Tempelopfer und ohne Priestertum. Die Pharisäer trachteten also danach, die jüdische Religion aus dem Tempel heraus dem Volk nahe zu bringen, in die Synagoge hinein und nach Hause. Daher gehen jüdische Liturgie und viele häusliche Rituale auf die Pharisäer zurück, ebenso die Interpretation des biblischen „Auge um Auge", die eben nicht als Vergeltung von Gleichem mit Gleichem, sondern vielmehr als Einlösung einer

---

[39] Marquard, S.186.
[40] Vgl. Baeck, *Harnack's Vorlesungen*, S. 25.

gerechten, angemessenen Kompensation für erlittenen Schaden verstanden werden muss.⁴¹

Weiterhin kritisiert Baeck Harnacks Weigerung, den Verlauf der politischen Ereignisse zu Jesu Lebzeiten mit in Betracht zu ziehen. Peter von der Osten-Sacken spricht hier von einem „Rückzug [...] aus der Geschichte" bei Harnack und merkt an, „wie protestantische Theologen sich einer konkreten historischen Erforschung des antiken Judentums entzogen und es zum Gegenbild ihrer Konzeption des Christentums stilisierten".⁴²

In der Gegenwart gibt es also sehr wohl auch kritische protestantische Stimmen, aber damals gab es auf Baecks Rezension wie auch auf andere damalige jüdische Proteste gegen Harnacks antijüdische Enterbungstheologie nicht eine einzige christliche Reaktion, weder von Harnack selbst, noch von anderen Theologen, die „in ihrer wissenschaftlichen Arbeit [...] die traditionellen Urteile über die jüdische Religion ungebrochen fortschrieben"⁴³ und eine jüdische Deutung der Person Jesu als Anmaßung empfanden. Für sie und für Harnack war das Judentum seit der Entstehung des Christentums obsolet geworden, und „eine gewisse systematische Verbohrtheit" und ein „ungebrochenes Überlegenheitsgefühl",⁴⁴ gepaart mit Erbitterung über die jüdische Anhänglichkeit an ihren Glauben, führten in christlichen Kreisen zu einer „Nichtwahrnehmung", zu einer „Verdrängung eines dem jüdischen Selbstverständnis angemessenen Wissens vom Jüdischen; einer Bemühung darum, eines Interesses daran, einer Offenheit dafür".⁴⁵ Die protestantischen Universitätsprofessoren nahmen die wissenschaftlichen Arbeiten ihrer jüdischen Kollegen einfach nicht zur Kenntnis und das Judentum nicht ernst,⁴⁶ während sich die jüdischen Gelehrten gegen verzerrte Darstellungen und Verunglimpfung ihrer Tradition wehrten und eine vorurteilsfreie Kenntnis des Judentums forderten.⁴⁷ Die höhnische Zurückweisung einer konkreten Auseinandersetzung und die Verweigerung jeglicher Wahrnehmung des jüdischen Standpunkts führten schließlich zu jenem politischen und theologischen Versagen, in dem die „verhängnisvolle Wirkungsgeschichte christlichen Redens über das Judentum überhaupt zum Tragen" kam.⁴⁸ Nicht nur war nach Wiese die Chance zu einem of-

---

⁴¹ Vgl. John D. Rayner. *The Truth about the Pharisees. The Evidence of the New Testament.* In: John D. Rayner. *Signposts to the Messianic Age. Sermons and Lectures.* London: Mitchell, 2006, S 144–152.
⁴² Vgl. Wiese, *Wissenschaft des Judentums*, S. 13.
⁴³ Ibd., S. 166.
⁴⁴ Marquard, S. 183.
⁴⁵ Wiese, *Wissenschaft des Judentums*, S. 154.
⁴⁶ Vgl. ibd., S. 18. Erst in der Weimarer Epoche änderte sich das.
⁴⁷ Vgl. ibd., S. 363.
⁴⁸ Ibd., S. 368.

fenen Gespräch für lange Zeit vertan. Die verschärfte Abgrenzung mitsamt ihrer Beharrung auf der Fremdheit und Minderwertigkeit des Judentums sollten bald darauf auf fatale Weise mentalitätsbildend wirken und die Vernichtungspolitik zumindest erleichtern.

Heute zeigen sich neue Wege auf, doch betont Wiese auch, dass es für die Juden immer noch Grund gäbe, Vereinnahmung zu befürchten, wenn christliche Theologen jüdische Themen aufgreifen. Die Judaistik dürfe nicht zur Magd der christlichen Theologie werden, sondern erreicht werden muss ihre eigenständige, gleichberechtigte Stellung im akademischen Diskurs.[49]

Marquard schrieb noch vor 20 Jahren, dass Leo Baecks Reaktion auf Harnack in ihren wichtigsten Aussagen zum größten Teil immer noch nicht integriert worden sei, weder in das Selbstverständnis des Christentums, noch in die christliche Sicht des Judentums.[50] Leo Baecks Buch über „das Wesen des Judentums" gilt als klassische Selbstaussage des modernen Judentums.

Die Bedeutung der Halacha ist von Christen oft fehlinterpretiert worden. Baeck betont, dass die Halacha, das Ritual im Judentum, nur als „Zaun um die Lehre" gedacht wird, doch sollte man den Zaun nicht für wichtiger halten als den Weinberg!

Baecks Buch beinhaltet keine Theorie über Gottes Verhältnis zum menschlichen Schicksal, keine Lehre über den Charakter der göttlichen Offenbarung, keine Geschichtstheologie. Stattdessen ist sein Thema des Menschen Suche nach Gott,[51] d.h. die Anstrengung, das Göttliche im eigenen Leben zu begreifen.

Während im Christentum der Mensch mit seiner Erbsünde ohne Christus hilflos dasteht, handelt der jüdische Mensch aus eigener Kraft. Während im Protestantismus die sittliche Tat nicht die eigene Arbeit des Menschen, sondern ein Geschenk Gottes ist, handelt der jüdische Mensch als freie sittliche Persönlichkeit. Hierbei soll die innere Gesetzgebung für die äußere Handlung gewissermaßen die Idee Gottes sein.

Leo Baeck formuliert das so: das verborgene Göttliche offenbart sich nicht selbst, sondern das Gebot: Gott ist nicht der offenbarte Gott, sondern der offenbarende Gott.[52] Baeck bleibt in der Tradition von Philo und Maimonides: Gott erkennen wir nicht, Gott ist nicht unser direktes Thema. Wir können nur das, was von

---

[49] Vgl. ibd., S. 369.
[50] Vgl. Marquard, S. 169.
[51] Vgl. Liebeschütz, S. 75.
[52] Vgl. Ernst Ludwig Ehrlich. *Leo Baeck. Der Mensch und sein Werk*. In: *Leo Baeck – Lehrer und Helfer in schwerer Zeit*. Werner Licharz (Hrsg.). Arnoldshainer Texte, 20. Frankfurt/Main: Haag & Herchen, 1983, S. 80–100, hier S. 84.

Gott ausgeht, erfahren: die Offenbarung ist Ethik, Handlungsanweisung. Das Bekenntnis zu der einen Gottheit, ehrfürchtig ausgedrückt im täglichen Gebet *Schema Jisrael*, ist verknüpft mit der Bereitschaft, sich für das göttliche Gebot der Ethik zu entscheiden: „Du sollst – so spricht der Ewige."

Das Gebot ist jedoch nicht nur starres Gesetz. Es kann leitend sein, ist aber nie für alle Zeit abgeschlossen, auch wenn man im Religiösen gerne angelangt sein möchte. Rechtgläubiger Stillstand kann zu moralischer Saturiertheit und zum Hochmut führen.[53] Leo Baeck führt aus, dass das Judentum keine Dogmen kennt und keine zentrale Autorität, so dass Freiheit des Denkens für jeden einzelnen Juden gegeben ist. Die Juden sind ein fragendes Volk, und damit verknüpft sich eine Mission, nämlich die Gerechtigkeit immer wieder aufs Neue einzufordern und daran zu arbeiten. Die jüdische Aufgabe bestehe darin, das Gewissen der Menschheit anzusprechen, und das bedeute eher Konfrontation als Anpassung.[54] Die Juden würden oft ein Nein aussprechen müssen um einer großen Forderung willen; es sei Aufgabe der Juden, in der Opposition zu stehen.

1948 äußerte sich Leo Baeck in einem überfüllten Hamburger Hörsaal zum vermeintlichen technischen Fortschritt. Er war der Ansicht, dass Fortschritte in der Technologie auf Kosten des moralischen Fortschrittes gemacht würden. Hoffnung für die Zukunft liege allein im menschlichen Gewissen, das sich zum Bewusstsein einer Gesamtverantwortung erweitern müsse.[55]

Leo Baeck verkörperte den modernen deutschen Rabbiner als Bildungsbürger und Akademiker. Sein neuer Aufgabenbereich lag immer noch, aber weniger in der Interpretation der Halacha, der religiösen Praxis, aber mehr noch in seiner Autorität als einer geistigen und moralischen Instanz,[56] die das partikularistische jüdische Anliegen mit einer universalistischen Perspektive in Einklang zu bringen vermochte.

Leo Baeck betrachtete das Judentum in all seiner Divergenz stets als eine Einheit. Innerhalb des Gesamtjudentums sollte das liberale Judentum „das lebendige Gewissen des Judentums" sein und Verständnis und Achtung aufbringen für die Tradition.[57] An der Spitze stehe die Ethik, die sich immer und gerade im Alltag bewähren müsse.

---

[53] Vgl. ibd., S. 85.

[54] Vgl. Michael A. Meyer. *Denken und Wirken Leo Baecks nach 1945*. In: *Leo Baeck 1873–1956. Aus dem Stamme von Rabbinern.* Georg Heuberger und Fritz Backhaus (Hrsg.). Frankfurt/Main: Jüdischer Verlag, 2001, S. 129–146, S. 132.

[55] Vgl. ibd., S. 141.

[56] Vgl. Rachel Heuberger. *Weshalb soll der Mensch nur eine Richtung haben? Leo Baecks Studium und Rabbinertätigkeit in den Jahren 1891 bis 1912*. In: *Leo Baeck 1873–1956. Aus dem Stamme von Rabbinern.* Georg Heuberger und Fritz Backhaus (Hrsg.). Frankfurt/Main: Jüdischer Verlag, 2001, S. 26–43, hier S. 32.

[57] Vgl. Ehrlich, S. 98f.

Dies mache die Dynamik der jüdischen Religion aus, die dem Menschen die Aufgabe zuweist, eine bessere Welt zu gestalten, basierend auf der Geschichte des Bundes zwischen Israel und der einen Gottheit. Diese Treue mache den jüdischen Glauben aus, so wie jenes Wort אמונה – *emuna*, das man gewöhnlich als „Glaube" übersetzt, eigentlich „Treue" bedeutet bzw. „zu etwas fest stehen", woher denn auch das Wort „Amen" abgeleitet ist.

Die Aufgabe des Juden formuliert Baeck auch in der Londoner Vorlesung, die den Individualismus im Judentum zum Thema hat. Es geht darum, aus der Individualität eine eigene, persönliche Antwort an Gott geben zu können, bzw. das „Du sollst" als das von Gott von Dir Geforderte zu akzeptieren und danach zu handeln.

Eingangs weist Leo Baeck auf die alten Griechen hin, auf deren Prometheus und Kassandra, aus deren heroischen Gestalten Individualität erwächst. Daneben habe das AT eine schlichtere Form der Individualität entwickelt und zwar in der Form des Gebotes: Du sollst das Gebot erfüllen. Ihr steht alle ohne Ausnahme vor dem Ewigen. In Deinem Herzen steht das Gebot. Es sind ganz einfache Worte, doch sei die Bedeutung revolutionär. Du, nicht ein Patrizier, jedes einfache Du, Du bist aufgerufen von dem einen Gott. Jeder Einzelne, in seiner Besonderheit, Unscheinbarkeit, ist angesprochen.

In der Verbindung von Gebot und Gebet tritt der verpflichtende Charakter des Gebotes für das Individuum auch stark zutage, denn im Gebet wird sich der Mensch des Gebotes bewusst.

Wenn es heißt: „Preise meine Seele, mein Ich, den Ewigen",[58] so sind das Worte des Einzelnen. Dem Menschen als Individuum ist die Ehre Gottes anvertraut.

Wenn auch das Beten und das Gebot jeden Menschen in seiner Individualität erfassen, so bleibt es jedoch nicht dabei, sondern es wird im jüdischen Denken Individualität ins Soziale hinein erweitert und in das Verhältnis von Mensch zu Mensch übertragen. Harnack hatte doch behauptet, dass erst seit Jesus Liebe und Nächstenliebe besondere Beachtung gefunden habe, doch steht schon bei Leviticus 19,18: וְאָהַבְתָּ לְרֵעֲךָ כָּמוֹךָ – *we-ahavta le-re'echa kamocha* – „Liebe Deinen Nächsten, denn er ist wie Du!"[59] So übersetzt Leo Baeck diese Stelle und fügt hinzu: „Die Individualität gewinnt ihre ganze Kraft, wenn sie Individualität ist um meinetwillen und zugleich um eines anderen willen."[60]

Abschließend bringt Leo Baeck noch einen Gedanken, der im Talmud diskutiert wird und der vielleicht der rührendste ist: Ein Mensch tritt Dir gegenüber. Du

---

[58] Leo Baecks Vortrag *Individualität im Judentum*, vgl. Fußnote 7.
[59] Ibd.
[60] Ibd.

weißt nicht, wer er ist. So ist es mit den Armen und Aussätzigen vor den Toren. Doch könnte einer von ihnen der Messias sein. Der Arme, der Unbedeutende, der Unbekannte, er ist ein Ich, und wer weiß, was aus ihm hervorgeht. Es gibt keine Kleinen, keinen Unbedeutenden. Ein Individuum ist auch er. Und wenn nur ein Einziger sich vertieft in das Heilige, dort weilt dann die göttliche Präsenz, auf Hebräisch die *Schechina* – שכינה.[61]

Jedes einzelne gerechte Individuum, auch wenn es noch so unbekannt und unscheinbar sein mag, kann die göttliche Präsenz in das menschliche Leben hineinbringen!

---

[61] Ibd.

Walter Homolka

Leo Baeck's Criticism on Martin Luther and its Purpose in a Search for Jewish Identity

Liberal Judaism and Protestant Liberal Thought

During the first decades of the Second Empire (1870–1914), an unprecedented relationship emerged within political liberalism based on its strong influences from liberal Protestantism on the one side[1] and from liberal Jewish society on the other. Liberal Jews and liberal Protestants seemed to share a common set of values as well as similar political goals.

Liberal Jewish theology – with spokesmen like Joseph Eschelbacher, Moritz Lazarus, Moritz Güdemann, Ludwig Geiger and Leo Baeck to name but a few – and liberal Protestant theology – represented by Ernst Troeltsch, Albert Ritschl, Martin Rade and Adolf von Harnack, among others – were both concerned with finding solutions to questions each of them raised in the same way. In searching for answers, they found themselves on common ground.

Both groups stressed the neo-Kantian ideal of human beings enabled by ethics to subject all life to an *a priori* system of principles. It can be said that liberal Protestantism and liberal Judaism tried in the same way to reinterpret religious traditions on the basis of modern rationality. And both attempted to purify their faith of irrational components.[2]

One decisive incongruence continued to separate liberal Jewish theology and liberal Protestant theology: the assertion by Christian theology that Christianity is superior to Judaism and the hypothesis that Judaism must have been quite a decadent faith even prior to Jesus.

The lectures of Adolf von Harnack on the "Essence of Christianity" (*Wesen des Christentums*), published in 1900, may be seen in this light; Judaism seems to be characterized as an initial and antiquated stage of religion that gave way to Christianity.

---

[1] For the development of Liberalism and the influences of liberal Protestant theology see: Uriel Tal. *Liberal Protestantism and the Jews in the Second Reich 1870–1914*. In: *Jewish Social Studies*, vol. 26, 1964, pp. 23–41.

[2] cf. ibid., pp. 35–36.

It is hardly surprising that Harnack's lectures drew heavy criticism from Jewish scholars, orthodox and liberal alike, immediately after their successful publication. One of the first Jewish reactions, however, came from Leo Baeck, who published a review of Harnack's book in the *"Monatsschrift für Geschichte und Wissenschaft des Judentums"*[3] in 1901. Using overt polemics Baeck tries to draw a sketch of the essence of Judaism by criticizing Christianity as presented by Harnack.

What are the main points of Baeck's criticism of Harnack's "Essence of Christianity"? Firstly, he decries the lack of appreciation for Jewish scholarship and literature. This, he criticizes, leads to a misinterpretation of Judaism in the time of Jesus. Secondly, Baeck demonstrates the apologetic intention of Harnack's book: to present Christianity in a most intriguing and positive light.

It is remarkable that it is through his argument with this liberal Protestant that Leo Baeck became known to a larger public. Harnack's book "Essence of Christianity" (*Wesen des Christentums*) inspired Baeck to write his *"Wesen des Judentums"* (Essence of Judaism). Four years' work went into its publication, and it offers a much more elaborate answer to Harnack's theories than his review did before. A second expanded edition of *"Wesen des Judentums"* followed in 1922, becoming the authoritative guide for subsequent editions.

Although neither Harnack nor Christianity is mentioned explicitly anywhere in the book, Baeck's intention is clear: "Essence of Judaism" is the apologetic answer to Harnack's "Essence of Christianity."

Baeck confronts Harnack's description of Judaism with the image of an "intellectually orientated" (*geistig*) Jewish faith defined by ethics and which is genuinely universal; the corresponding piety emphasizes good deeds and trust. The essence of Judaism, according to Baeck, lies in the ethical monotheism of the prophets.

The struggle against Harnack's theses may well be seen as the starting point of Baeck's interest in Christianity, which would remain his continuing concern. From that point, Baeck's interest in Christianity as the counterpart to Jewish theology is present throughout all of his works. Baeck's body of writings contains more than thirty titles on the relationship between Judaism and Christianity. Seventeen of them were published in the Weimar Republic, five of the most important works even during the Third Reich.[4] One may say that the work of Leo Baeck is charac-

---

[3] *Monatsschrift für Geschichte und Wissenschaft des Judentums*, vol. 45, 1901, pp. 97–120.

[4] Theodore Wiener. *The Writings of Leo Baeck*. In: *Studies in Bibliography and Booklore*, vol. 1.3, 1954; see also Robert Raphael Geis. *Versuche des Verstehens. Dokumente jüdisch-christlicher Begegnung aus den Jahren 1918–1933*. Theologische Bücherei, 33. München: Kaiser, 1966, p. 50.

terized by a permanent discussion with Christianity, even in most difficult times like the Third Reich.

Leo Baeck's Model of Polarity

One general methodological approach to criticizing Christianity is present in all of Baeck's works. He perpetually develops a polarized model that sets "classical" and "romantic" religion in opposition to one another; the same holds true for their corresponding elements of "mystery" (*Geheimnis*) and *"commandment"* (Gebot), i.e. "mystics" and "ethics". An analysis of this polarity as determined by these criteria provides a prism through which to compare the Judaism and Christianity as religions.

Speaking of Christianity, Baeck identifies and distinguishes two main streams of tradition: Paul, Augustine and Martin Luther represent the element of mystery; Jesus, Pelagius and Calvin are identified with the element of commandment. "Classical religion" (i.e. Judaism) is readily described as a perfect balance between mystery and commandment; Christianity is predominantly shaped by St. Paul and Luther and therefore described as "romantic religion" per se.

Are there any sources of contemporary thought that might shed light on the origin of Baeck's model? The terms "mystery" and "commandment" should really be seen in the context of the renaissance of mysticism in the 1920s and the ongoing scholarly interest in mystics. Furthermore, we can assert an influence by the debate on natural law (*Naturrechtsdebatte*) and its impact on the development of social ethics in post-enlightenment times. This debate was of special interest for Protestant scholars and undoubtedly had some resonance in a Judaism heavily influenced by Hegelian and Neo-Kantian thought.

Leo Baeck's Exposition of the Teachings of Martin Luther

Baeck develops his typology by concentrating on the theology of Martin Luther and its Pauline sources. It is striking that Baeck is mainly interested in two issues within Luther's theology: the question of *liberum* or *servum arbitrium*, i.e. whether human beings possess a free or a bound will, and the doctrine of the Two Kingdoms.

Baeck presents the reader with an image of Lutheranism that is deeply influenced by the Prussian Protestant state church (*Staatskirche*), and the Jewish perception of this alliance of Protestant Church and State. The description of Luther's theology is in many respects a critical one; Baeck's critique is also frequently marked by one-sidedness and prejudice. In the following description I intend to give a structured outline of Baeck's understanding of Martin Luther's thoughts –

focusing on the constitution of the Individual before God. It must be kept in mind that Luther did not present a systematic theology in the ordinary sense; there is also no doubt that my summary will in itself bear an interpretation of what I think that Baeck understood when he refers to Luther's words. In any case, I shall try to remain faithful to Baeck's wording in order to make my reconstruction as accurate as possible.

The Individual and Original Sin

According to Baeck's interpretation of Luther's views, original sin is the determining force and the unyielding definition of humankind. Sin is not in any person, but rather the person is within original sin. Neither the individual nor humanity as a whole caused original sin, nor do they have the ability to remove it. Mortals are at the mercy of original sin. Because sin is so integral to the nature of humankind, only an act beyond this realm of nature – that is, a miracle – can eliminate sin. Thus, sin is overcome through God's grace, through a redeemer."[5] In this interpretation, however, it seems to Baeck that the individual is condemned to a totally passive role. In this way, religion becomes redemption from the will and liberation from the deed.[6]

Commandment and Grace

It is somewhat awkward that Baeck refers to Matthew 5:18 and Gal. 3:24 in attempting to explain the Pauline understanding of the law. Before redemption, the Biblical law remained basically valid. In Christ, redemption has finally taken place. Therefore, to postulate any further obligatory nature of the law would undermine this salvatory act.[7] By denying law any essential significance, Baeck sees Paul and Luther as doing more than just opposing it as ceremonial; "Whoever expects the good from the fulfillment of the commandments and duties, still lives under the yoke of the law."[8]

Previously, darkness was all that surrounded the spirit; now divine grace guarantees to show the light that guides humankind to its prescribed goal: to become perfected individuals.[9] Those who judge themselves as just will find themselves

---

[5] Leo Baeck. *Romantic Religion.* In: *Judaism and Christianity. Essays.* Philadelphia: Jewish Publication Society of America, 1958, pp. 243f.

[6] Leo Baeck. *Aus drei Jahrtausenden. Wissenschaftliche Untersuchungen und Abhandlungen zur Geschichte des jüdischen Glaubens.* Tübingen: Mohr, 1958, p. 123.

[7] Ibid., p. 205.

[8] Baeck, *Romantic Religion*, p. 249.

[9] Ibid., pp. 206, 210.

on the path leading away from justice. To Baeck's mind Luther expresses it as follows: one mustn't "befoul oneself" with the law.[10]

The law is surpassed by faith in Jesus Christ as the Redeemer and of no real value anymore in the process of gaining redemption.[11] For Baeck, this means the rejection of individual moral freedom and the ability to actively embrace the good.

Righteousness Solely on the Basis of Faith

Christian righteousness flows from faith in the son of God – *Justitia christiana est fiducia in Filium Dei*.[12] It is not the same as righteous action[13] because Christ fulfilled the law for humankind.[14] And the Gospel is a doctrine which does not rely on observance of the law: *"Est ergo evangelium doctrina talis quae nullam legem admittit."*[15] Baeck draws the conclusion that like Paul, Luther supported both the notion of unconditional original sin[16] and the totality of divine grace,[17] corresponding to a complete passivity on the part of humanity.[18] The individual cannot find God, God has to find him, Baeck says.[19] Placing all emphasis on salvation, Luther seems to deny any value of deeds and human action. There is no room left, Baeck claims, for individual moral action and the ability to shape the world.[20]

---

[10] Ibid. p. 242, quoted from *Dr. Martin Luther's sämmtliche Werke*. Erlangen: Heyder, 1826ff, henceforth cited in this manner: "Erl."; *Dr. Martin Luther's Werke. Kritische Gesamtausgabe. Weimarer Ausgabe*. Weimar: Böhlau, 1883ff, here vol. 17 I, p. 111, henceforth cited in this manner: WA 17 I, p. 111: "Also das ein rein hertz haben nicht allein heisse nichts unreins gedencken, sondern wenn durch Gottes wort das gewissen erleucht und sicher wird, das sichs nicht besuddelt am gesetz. Also das ein Christen wisse, das yhm nicht schadet, ob er es halte odder nicht, und thuet wol, das sonst verbotten ist, odder lessit, das sonst geboten ist, ist yhm keins suende, Denn er kan keine thun, weil das hertz reine ist."

[11] WA 40 I, p. 672: "Quare credentibus in Christum tota lex abrogata est."

[12] WA 40 I, p. 366: "Christiana iustitia coram deo est credere in filium. Sic Abraham in semen. vel fides est fiducia cordis per Christum in Deum.' Baeck quotes from Erl. I, p. 334: "[...] christianam justitiam proprie ac diserte sic definire, quod sit fiducia in filium Dei, seu fiducia cordis per Christum in Deum."

[13] Baeck, *Romantic Religion*, p. 84.

[14] WA 1, p. 105.

[15] Erl. II, p. 113. However in WA 40 I, p. 141: "Ideo Evangelium solum revelat filium Dei. Est ergo doctrina vel cognitio in qua nulla penitus lex est."

[16] Leo Baeck. *Judentum in der Kirche*. In: *Aus drei Jahrtausenden*, p. 134; 12. WA 42, p. 106.

[17] WA 24, p. 244. "Es mus von hymel und allein aus gnaden komen, das Gott durch die verheissung des Euangelions das hertz trifft, das es fuelet und muesse sagen, das es vor nye bedacht odder ynn synn genomen habe, das yhm solche gnade solt widderfaren."

[18] WA 6, p. 530; WA 2, p. 420; cf. Leo Baeck. *Epochen der jüdischen Geschichte*. Stuttgart: Kohlhammer, 1974, p. 119. "Recte ergo dixi, oportere ergo hominem de suis operibus diffidere et velut paralyticum remissis manibus et pedibus gratiam operum artificem implorare."

[19] Baeck, *Romantic Religion*, p. 204.

[20] Leo Baeck. *Wege im Judentum. Aufsätze und Reden*. Berlin: Schocken, 1933, p. 385.

Salvation by faith is also determined right from the outset[21] so that morality lacks any religious purpose. Baeck cites Luther: "I live as I live; that does not make the doctrine false. We must not consider and judge the life, but the doctrine. Even if the life is not so pure, the doctrine can remain pure nevertheless, and one can be content with the life."[22]

"By faith alone" could only possibly mean the following for Luther: without action, even anti-action: "You do not owe it to God to do anything except believe and profess. In all other matters he releases you and leaves you free to do as you please without any danger of conscience."[23]

This reads as though the more sin there is, the more opportunity for God's divine grace to prove its strength. In this context Baeck sees Luther's famous recommendation to Melanchthon of *"fortiter pecca"* (sin bravely) in 1521. To Baeck this appears to be by no means ironic, but, on the contrary, deeply imbued with Pauline doctrine.[24]

We may question here whether or not Luther's concept is really identical with Paul's. Christian Luther studies have been successfully endeavoring for decades to present us with a considerably more differentiated picture of the two thinkers. However, Baeck's fervor may again be a product of the highly structured way in which he juxtaposes classical and romantic elements within religions. In any case, Luther himself did in other places offer explanations about action, for example in his *"Sermon von den guten Werken."* Truly, humankind's only viable action in its relationship to God can be faith. This faith, however, constitutes the freedom to act in whatever way is required.

It is thus quite important to note the priority of conscience within the acquired state of faith. In some respects Baeck and Luther may not even be so far apart in their approach to everyday moral behavior as it would seem at first glance. Strictly speaking, the dividing line really emerges when the question of redemption arises: whether or not God had to send Jesus Christ as the driving force of humankind's salvation, and whether or not the old path of biblical commandment could retain its validity. This question is at the heart of Judaism's identity crisis

---

[21] Baeck, *Romantic Religion*, pp. 203f., cf. p. 85; WA 24, p.18: "Denn ein solch mensch mus allen dingen gestorben seyn, dem guten und bösen, dem tod und leben, der hell und dem hymel und von hertzen bekennen, das er aus eygnen krefften nichts vermag."; *Die Deutsche Bibel*. D. Martin Luthers Werke. Kritische Gesamtausgabe. Weimarer Ausgabe, vol. 9. Weimar: Böhlau, 1955, p. 23, henceforth cited in this manner "DB, p. 23": "Zu Rom. 9–11": "leret er von der ewigen Versehung Gottes, Daher es ursprunglich fleusset, wer gleuben, oder nicht gleuben sol, von suenden los, oder nicht los werden kann. Damit es je gar aus unsern henden genomen, und alleine in Gottes hand gestellet sey, das wir frum werden."

[22] Baeck, *Romantic Religion*, p. 252; WA 24, p. 607 (falsely cited by Baeck as p. 606).

[23] WA 12, p. 131; cf. WA 17 I, p. 111.

[24] Baeck, *Romantic Religion*, p. 252.

since Paul. Baeck enters the Jewish-Christian battlefield armed with Enlightenment ideas when he focuses on the value and priority of moral action based on an individual free will.

Free Will

To Baeck it is obvious: the faith of the lame as they await healing is no expression of deep conviction and of certainty. Baeck points out that in his view true insight works *within* the individual, rather than being brought into existence *by* the individual.[25] And, as there is no active choice for faith and healing in Christianity, there is no choice concerning the will, for the will of the individual is always the will to sin.[26] The human being can do nothing but sin.[27] There is no allowance for a gradual approach to the truth. The flow of grace alone gives the individual the sum of knowledge and total insight.[28] So, romantic religion really asks for the sacrifice of the intellect. In Luther's words: "In all who have faith in Christ reason shall be killed; else faith does not govern them; for reason fights against faith."[29] With this, knowledge must make itself subordinate to faith: *credo quia absurdud* – I believe because it is absurd.

At the instant of receiving faith, the individual is like a mere tool in the hands of a higher power.[30] Life is heteronomy, and at the same time, the omniscient and the blind face each other irreconcilably.

Salvation to a State of Grace through Word and Sacrament

Following out Baeck's line of thought, it is quite logical that happiness or grace is posited as the epitome of a fulfilled Christian life, the rhyme and reason of being. This state of grace clearly comes from divine grace and not as a result of moral action. Faith that does not require the completion of any tasks set by God refers back to the self and therefore becomes a yearning for bliss.[31] The individual asks selfishly if, when, and how redemption will be granted. This leads to a "sentimen-

---

[25] WA 10 I 2, p. 29: "Darumb lerne hie auß dem Evangelio, wie es tzugehet, wenn gott ansehet uns frum tzu machen, und wilchs der anfang sey, frum tzu werden. Es ist keyn ander anfang, denn das deyn konig tzu dyr kome und fahe ynn dyr an [...]".

[26] However, cf. Kant's "You can because you ought to" in Baeck, *Romantic Religion*, p. 254.

[27] WA 10 I2, p. 29: "[...] du kanst nichts denn sundigen, thu wie du wilt. [...] und must sundigen, wo du alleyn wirckst auß freyem willen."

[28] Baeck, *Romantic Religion*, p. 205.

[29] Ibid., p. 207 (quoted from Erlangen edition); see WA 47, p. 328.

[30] Baeck, *Romantic Religion*, p. 208.

[31] Ibid., p. 285 f.

tal brooding about sinfulness,"[32] as often seems typical of Protestantism, making it, Baeck writes, a doctrine of the salvation of the self. The sacraments offer this self-assurance, creating the individual's state of grace.[33] Bread, wine and holy water become supernatural substances through which faith flows and the individual is transformed, purified and renewed.[34] On the other hand, Baeck cites the Reformer Kaspar Schwenckfeld, who reproaches Luther, saying that he "will not let anybody become blessed without an external thing."[35]

In Baeck's eyes baptism and Holy Communion are not just symbols for Luther, but rather supernatural realities. And the same is the case with the word of God. This word does not merely mean something; it is significant and effective in itself and solely by being preached. "That you should hear and receive the word is not by your strength, but by the grace of God which makes the gospel bear fruit in you that you may have faith in it."[36]

As the constitution of faith, the word descends upon humanity; and without any action on their part, human beings are brought to accept it. Through word and sacrament, they are taken and placed within the realm of salvation, no longer asking what tasks they are to do, but whether redemption has already been granted.

Baeck's View of the Constitution of the Individual before God

As shown above, Luther's teachings about the individual's constitution before God are viewed by Baeck as a state of passivity, as mere waiting for God's grace. This stands in direct opposition to Baeck's understanding of human responsibility and his concept of life. According to Baeck, the meaning of life consists of two spiritual experiences that are joined together in Judaism: the mystery and the commandment.[37] Through the mystery, the individual is shown the deeper reality hidden below the surface of one's life and becomes aware that he was created and brought into being – i.e. conscious of an undetectable and, at the same time, protective power. He experiences that which embraces him and all things. He experi-

---

[32] Ibid., p. 278.

[33] Baeck, *Romantic Religion*, p. 225.

[34] WA 6, p. 538: "Sicut enim verbum dei potens erst, dum sonat, etiam impii cor immutare, quod non minus est surdum et incapax quam ullus parvulus, ita per orationem Ecclesiae offerentis et credentis, cui omnia possibilia sunt, et parvulus fide infusa mutatur, mundatur et renovatur." (falsely cited by Baeck as p. 539).

[35] Baeck, *Romantic Religion*, p. 226.

[36] Ibid., p. 22; see Erl. 10 (2), 12.

[37] Leo Baeck. *Geheimnis und Gebot*. In: *Wege im Judentum. Aufsätze und Reden*. Berlin: Schocken, 1933, pp. 33–48; henceforth cited according to the English translation *Mystery and Commandment*. In: *Judaism and Christianity. Essays by Leo Baeck*. Philadelphia: Jewish Publication Society, 1958, pp. 171–85.

ences, in the words of the ancient metaphor in the Blessing of Moses, "the arms of eternity."[38]

While the mystery raises the question of the meaning of life, the commandment raises the question of its goal. The commandment is the unconditional demand that challenges a human being[39] Pressuring, victorious, absolute and independent, the commandment passes from generation to generation on into the future.[40] It is grounded in the being, the eternal, the unfathomable, and it appears to humanity as that which blesses, is creative and is fertile.[41] "The realm of the commandment is a realm of revelation and as such a realm of grace."[42]

It is Baeck's firm belief that both mystery and commandment come from the one God and neither can exist without the other. Without the certainty of God's existence as a mystery, there can be a moral structure consisting of teachings of wisdom and counsels of reason, but the unchangeable and categorical nature of the commandment would remain unfathomable for humanity.[43] The mystery and the experience of faith is that which gives birth to a religion. It may be the beginning of religion but it is not the whole story, just as birth is not the entirety one's life.[44]

Faith and freedom in Judaism, according to Baeck, need the tension between the poles of mystery and commandment, for the infinite appears in the finite, and whatever is finite bears witness to the infinite.[45] Such a relationship between mysticism and ethics is not one of conflict, but represents a necessary combination on the way to God. For Baeck the goal of life is righteousness before God: through work and achievement, through the fulfillment of one's duty and the struggle for the commandment. Rather than creating a clear conscience, religion should constantly unsettle and challenge it. Only then can it really be religion. It must be able and determined to offer resistance to every power possible, in the name of defending the eternal.[46]

---

[38] Ibid., p. 171.
[39] Leo Baeck. *Zwischen Wittenberg und Rom.* In: *Wege im Judentum. Aufsätze und Reden.* Berlin: Schocken, 1933, pp. 270–87, here p. 280.
[40] Baeck, *Mystery and Commandment,* p. 178 f.
[41] Ibid., p. 179.
[42] Leo Baeck. *Dieses Volk. Jüdische Existenz.* 2 vol. Frankfurt/Main: Europäische Verlagsanstalt, 1955–1957, here vol. 1, p. 103.
[43] Baeck, *Wege im Judentum,* p. 280.
[44] Baeck, *Romantic Religion,* p. 210.
[45] Baeck, *Mystery and Commandment,* p. 175.
[46] Baeck, *Zwischen Wittenberg und Rom,* p. 287.

To Baeck, the religious consciousness is molded by the experience of closeness to God, not by a special status relative to God enjoyed by some individuals on the basis of divine grace.[47] Human beings live in humility before God, in full knowledge of their absolute dependence and with a reverence for an ethically superior that demands and directs,[48] that speaks and requires a reply – man's decision – and that brings them joy.[49]

According to Baeck, human life exists in the tension between desire and duty. "Ye shall be unto me a kingdom of priests and a holy nation" is a phrase that has acquired in Judaism the character of a religious confession.[50] Faith does not turn away from the world. It does not await salvation from the world and its days. On the contrary, it is faith in the world and the certainty that all possible opposites will be reconciled. It is redemption not from the world, but in the world. This world should be sanctified and therefore raised up to the Kingdom of God. The Holy and the Profane are therefore inseparably joined. In essence, there is no mundane life; nothing is the mere world, God is in everything.[51] He permeates the whole of life. All future is a future of the commandments – a future in which they are realized and fulfilled,[52] that thrives through the path they take, not through miracles, myth or fate. In the days of the Messianic age, the spirit of God will live unchallenged in the hearts of humanity. At that time all commandments and obligations will cease to exist, for duty will have become part of the innermost nature of the individual. God's will shall become our own and in that sense, our will shall become one with the divine will.[53]

Religion and State

The Lutheran State Church

To understand Baeck's critical views on Luther's teaching of the "Two Kingdoms" and the "Kingdom of God," we must first make a short survey of the Lutheran church in Prussia as experienced by Baeck. Leo Baeck sees the "police state making all decisions for the people" as developing directly from Lutheranism. Coin-

---

[47] Leo Baeck. *The Essence of Judaism*. 6th edn. London: Macmillan, 1936, pp. 44f.
[48] Baeck, *Wege im Judentum*, p. 34.
[49] Baeck, *Dieses Volk*, vol. 1, p. 57.
[50] Baeck, *The Essence of Judaism*, p. 45.
[51] Baeck, *Mystery and Commandment*, p. 292.
[52] Baeck, *Romantic Religion*, p. 120.
[53] Ibid., p. 241.

ing the term, Baeck says it has become the "Prussian religion," combining an inflexible sense of authority and subject with a Christian world view. In this constellation ethics are relegated solely to the private sphere.[54]

With its church state and state church, the ruling sovereign of the state being at the same time the *summus episcopus* (highest bishop) of the Protestant church, Lutheranism had a decisive influence in Prussia and represented a conservative, one is even tempted to call it "destructive" power. Contemporary opposition to this development was the driving force behind the Enlightenment and Kantian philosophy.[55] Through such a connection to the state, Lutheranism declined to represent a universal message, missing its chance to become a world religion. The idea of the kingdom of God took on a secondary role to the confessional state.

Baeck refers quite simplistically to Ernst Troeltsch's term "Christian society" as the goal of Protestant efforts, which had actually been used far earlier by F.J. Stahl and the conservative *"Kreuzzeitung."*[56] However, with the church being taken over by the state, what began as a protest took on a rather non-Protestant end.

Baeck sees the period following the First World War as a turning point of Protestantism. The revolution of 1918 was an unexpected shock for the Protestant church.[57] Not only did the alliance with the state fall apart, the Protestant church was forced to come to an agreement with the democratic or even revolutionary powers of the new democracy. The Protestant church lost its state support and at the same time, a living piece of its certainty and ideals.[58]

The State as the purpose of history (Hegel), Baeck claims, never represented a doctrine of faith or a justification.[59] Following the collapse of the old meaning of the State,[60] it seemed to Baeck that Protestantism needed not only a new means of support, but also new content. But how did this connection between throne and altar develop? Leo Baeck sees the roots in Luther's teachings of two kingdoms.

---

[54] Baeck, *Wege im Judentum*, p. 386.

[55] Ibid., p. 384.

[56] Leo Baeck. *Volksreligion und Weltreligion. In: Wege im Judentum. Aufsätze und Reden.* Berlin: Schocken, 1933, pp. 195–207, here p. 204. See also Richard Rothe's works in the second half of the nineteenth century.

[57] See Hans-Walter Krumwiede. *Evangelische Kirche und Theologie in der Weimarer Republik.* Grundtexte zur Kirchen- und Theologiegeschichte, 2. Neukirchen-Vluyn, 1990, p. 10.

[58] Baeck, *Wege im Judentum*, p. 271.

[59] Ibid., pp. 271f.

[60] Ibid., p. 383.

On Luther's "Two Kingdoms": The Individual between Church and State

The teaching of the "two kingdoms" is one of the most important and at the same time one of the most disputed aspects of Lutheran theology. Its importance derives from focusing on the basic distinction of law and gospel. This, however, fosters a tendency to isolate spheres that actually belong together and, by this, isolating political life from ethical norms.[61] It is my intention to give a short introduction to the doctrine of the "two kingdoms" and then focus on Baeck's interpretation.

In a classical sense, Augustine had already divided the living sphere of human beings into two realms. Through birth, the individual is placed into the world of the mundane, the *"civitas terrana,"* a world determined by calculation, counting and weighing. The unfathomable grace of God is the sole vehicle for individuals to enter the *"civitas die,"* the sphere of God. But only the few are chosen; the masses, the *"massa perditionis,"* are condemned to eternal death. The human being is relegated in this view to the earthly sphere, and only through the passive fact of being chosen can the individual be lifted beyond this sphere by God's hand. The two kingdoms stand in opposition and only the miracle of divine election can raise an individual from the lower to the higher realm.[62] Baeck sees Luther as directly dependent on Augustine. In his view Luther appears to be primarily Augustine's student and successor.[63] Luther even, so he assumes, intensifies the teachings of the individual's total dependence on the mercy of God *"sicut cadaver"*: the individual must await the grace of God passively, like a corpse. As election lies outside the realm of human decision and freedom and the individual is condemned on the basis of original sin until touched by God's grace, the human community must therefore be based on social constraints. According to Baeck, there is neither motivation[64] nor even the opportunity for free, independent moral action.

Baeck cites a well-known quotation from the Middle Ages: *"homo est animal bipes quod vult cogi"* – the individual is a two-legged being that needs to be subjected to force.[65] This world of the lost and the rejected can be ruled only by violence. Even on the basis of its own assumptions, Lutheranism was, to Baeck's mind, never in the position of creating a system of ethics founded on religion.[66]

---

[61] A complete discussion of the teaching of the "two kingdoms" is given in *Reich Gottes und Welt: Die Lehre Luthers von den zwei Reichen*. Heinz-Horst Schrey (ed.). Wege der Forschung, 107, Darmstadt: Wissenschaftliche Buchgesellschaft, 1969, p. IX.

[62] Leo Baeck. *Epochen der jüdischen Geschichte*, pp. 118f.

[63] Leo Baeck. *Judentum in der Kirche*, p. 133: "die katholische Kirche dagegen 'kam doch immer wieder zu einem duldenden Einvernehmen mit einer Art von Semi-Pelagianismus.'"

[64] Baeck, *Wege im Judentum*, p. 385.

[65] Baeck, *Epochen der jüdischen Geschichte*, p. 120.

[66] Baeck, *Aus drei Jahrtausenden*, pp. 135f.

For Baeck, Luther's secular world is the place for morality. As *the "custos utriusque tabulae,"*[67] the ruling sovereign had within his disciplinary powers the responsibility to enforce matters of morality. In this way the individual was assigned to two spheres. On the one hand was the "spiritual individual" who had faith, and on the other hand was the "civil individual" who kept the commandments. Baeck saw this division as the inherent religious and ethical weakness of Luther's doctrine. Morality is that which the authorities demand.

Moral demands are thus no longer commandments or categorical imperatives, but mere directions: either decrees of the constituted authorities or "counsels of the conscience" of those who have heard a call. The doctrine of morality becomes a doctrine of individual cases, and the study or science of it approximates jurisprudence and becomes a matter of interpretation and legality.[68]

But that is not all. Luther established his church with the assistance of the secular rulers, and it became more and more based on the authority and the protection of the State.[69] A visible Church and State are joined in Lutheranism.[70] This sort of religion cannot exist without the State, for the authority of the State and of the Church lie in the same hands. The ruling sovereign is at the same time the head of the Church. As such, the State is granted absolute rule.[71] "Let every soul be subject unto the higher powers," for they reign by authority of God's commandment.[72]

Luther appears in Baeck's characterization to be filled with a deep pessimism regarding the world in its sinful state.[73] This corresponds to an inflexible and fatalistic sense of subservience, of subordination of social classes as a divine institution. The human being must be resigned to accepting the life and work circumstances he or she is born into. One is not allowed to tamper with the rigid barriers of caste and guild. Dependence and class as willed by God represent strict Lutheran thought.[74] The motivation for social progress is lacking, and work and cul-

---

[67] An expression used by Melanchthon, cf. Baeck, *Wege im Judentum*, p. 386 and *Dieses Volk*, vol. 1, p. 103.

[68] Baeck, *Romantic Religion*, pp. 267f.

[69] Baeck, *Wege im Judentum*, pp. 384f.

[70] Leo Baeck. *Helfer und Lehrer. Über Mittelalter und neue Zeit*. In: *Wege im Judentum. Aufsätze und Reden*. Berlin: Schocken, 1933, pp. 401–22, here p. 403.

[71] Baeck, *Aus drei Jahrtausenden*, p. 136.

[72] Leo Baeck. *Spinozas erste Einwirkungen auf Deutschland*. Inaugural Dissertation an der Friedrich-Wilhelms-Universität Berlin. Berlin: Mayer & Müller, 1895, p. 8; and Baeck, *Romantic Religion*, pp. 213f. This is almost a quote from Romans 13:1.

[73] Baeck, *Wege im Judentum*, p. 387.

[74] Baeck, *Romantic Religion*, p. 213; and Baeck, *Wege im Judentum*, p. 385.

tural life are devalued.[75] The principle of being "complete" discourages any advancement.

Baeck denounces Luther's lack of optimism as the most significant evil in his interpretation of the individual's role between State and Church. If the Messiah has already come and salvation has already been granted, then any hope for the future loses its meaning to a large degree and any urge to shape and better the world lacks a goal.[76]

The "Kingdom of God" according to Leo Baeck

In view of the Lutheran State-Church alliance, Leo Baeck poses what he considers the highest questions of truth and freedom: does religion assist in achieving a "clear conscience" by making a pact with all forms of power, even evil ones, for the sake of the demands of present? Or is religion capable of resisting and determined to resist for the sake of eternity?[77]

Baeck refers to the two realms and says that they do not oppose each other, but are intertwined, for "the one realm should penetrate the other, influencing and determining it."[78] The higher realm continually enters the lower one in the form of the commandment to touch humankind. The commandment includes goodness, devotion, selflessness, faith and reconciliation. "Being chosen" does not involve passivity, of being chosen by divine grace, but rather an active acceptance of God's call: "Now if you obey me fully and keep my covenant, then out of all nations you will be my treasured possession. For mine is the whole earth."[79]

This depicts the freedom of the individual very clearly. Each person has the ability to seize or to abandon the chance to be chosen, according to his or her own will. The commandment grasps individuals in the earthly realm and assists them in lifting themselves to the higher one. Both worlds are connected to each other, as expressed in the second section of the *Amidah* prayer: "[...] to order the world through the Kingdom of the Almighty." The kingdom of God, therefore, enters the earthly realm, so that the realm to come can begin for the people in the here and now. The dawn of the future starts in the present. Each individual must make

---

[75] Only the rejection of monastic idleness moved Luther to show some esteem for secular work.

[76] Baeck, *Romantic Religion*, pp. 285 f.; and Baeck, *Aus drei Jahrtausenden*, p. 136.

[77] Baeck, *Wege im Judentum*, p. 287.

[78] Baeck, *Epochen der jüdischen Geschichte*, pp. 119 ff. See more closely Luther's idea of "Königsherrschaft Christi" (Christ as King of both heavenly and earthly spheres); Ernst Wolf. *Die Königsherrschaft Christi und der Staat*. In: Werner Schmauch and Ernst Wolf. *Königsherrschaft Christi. Der Christ im Staat, Theologische Existenz heute*. Neue Serie, 64. München, 1958 pp. 20–61.

[79] Ex. 19:5.

his or her way to the higher realm, however, wherever he or she is at that moment. Deutero-Isaiah appeals for this in his call "Clear the way!"[80]

All action should be taken for the sake of God and not the State. Absolute independence of religion from the State is to Baeck's mind extremely significant. The Lutheran Reformation, however, placed religion in the hands of the State.[81] It is not difficult to note that in the context of the Weimar Republic Baeck's view is concentrated on conservative Lutheranism with its mentality of perseverance and grievance over the abdication of the monarchic system. The full picture emerges only when one includes cultural Protestantism, which must be considered as a notable minority within the Protestant spectrum of the Weimar Republic in terms of influence on the German church up until now.

Representatives such as Otto Baumgarten, Martin Rade or Hermann Mulert welcomed the revolution of 1918 and the emerging Weimar Republic as an opportunity for the church to liberate itself from the alienating alliance with the state. The theological and ecclesiastical consequences gave a chance for redirection towards the actual goals of Protestantism.

Leo Baeck: Representative of Jewish Theology?

Leo Baeck's picture of Judaism comes, on the one hand, from the spirit of rabbinical tradition and, on the other hand, from the patterns of thought of his time. It is particularly conspicuous how often Baeck uses the terminology of Immanuel Kant in the continuation of Jewish neo-Kantianism.[82] He speaks of "moral action" (*sittliches Handeln*),[83] of "heteronomy" (*Heteronomie*),[84] of striving for "bliss" (*Glückseligkeit*) as an antithesis to "morality" (*Sittlichkeit*),[85] and of "ad-

---

[80] Isa. 40:3; Baeck, *Epochen der jüdischen Geschichte*, p. 124.

[81] Ibid., p. 100.

[82] For another example of Jewish-Kantian synthesis see Friedrich W. Niewöhner. *Isaac Breuer und Kant: Ein Beitrag zum Thema ‚Kant und das Judentum'*. In: *Neue Zeitschrift für systematische Theologie und Religionsphilosophie*, vol. 17, 1975, pp. 142–50 and 19.2, 1977, pp. 172–85.

[83] Immanuel Kant. *Kritik der Urteilskraft*. Karl Vorländer (ed.). Reprint of 1924. Hamburg: Meiner, 1974, § 29 Allgemeine Anmerkung.

[84] Immanuel Kant. *Grundlegung zur Metaphysik der Sitten*. Reprint of the 3rd edition. Leipzig: Meiner, 1947, 2. Abschnitt; also *Kritik der praktischen Vernunft*. Karl Vorländer (ed.). Reprint of the 9th edition. Leipzig: Meiner, 1951, 1. Teil, 1. Buch, 1. Hauptstück, § 8, Lehrsatz IV.

[85] Immanuel Kant. *Kritik der reinen Vernunft*. Raymund Schmidt (ed.). Reprint of the 1st and 2nd edition. Hamburg: Meiner, 1971, Methodenlehre, 2. Hauptstück, 2. Absatz, also *Kritik der praktischen Vernunft*, 1. Teil, 1. Buch, 1. Hauptstück, § 8, Anmerkung II and ibid., 1. Teil, 2. Buch, 2. Hauptstück, V, also *Die Religion innerhalb der Grenzen der bloßen Vernunft*, Vorrede zu 1. Aufl., 1. Anmerkung and ibid., 1. Stück, Allgemeine Anmerkungen, 2. Anmerkung, also *Metaphysik der Sitten*. Karl Vorländer (ed.). Reprint of the 4th edition. Leipzig: Meiner, 1945, Einleitung II.

vice for the conscience" (*Gewissensratschläge*),[86] the "commandments of practical reason" (*Gebote der praktischen Vernunft*)[87] and the "categorical imperative" (*kategorischer Imperativ*).[88]

All in all, Jewish neo-Kantianism seems to conflict with the thought and background of the Christian Reformation. Beyond that, the aforementioned arguments and examples show how rarely Baeck touches the reality of Reformation thought, which is much more complex and dialectical. Nor does Baeck seem sensitive to the inherent tensions within Luther's terminology. This also raises the question as to what extent Baeck's reasoning is referring to Jewish tradition, though he must first be cleared of the accusation that he argues simply in the philosophical manner of the Enlightenment. Rather one could say that he uses this system of contemporary thought and its terminology in order to present his Jewish standpoint.

Leo Baeck's Assumptions about Luther

Leo Baeck presents a picture of Lutheran theology from a Jewish perspective that appears quite intriguing, especially for the Jewish intelligentsia he was trying to convince. Nevertheless, I have indicated before that one might well be right to ask if Baeck was capable of presenting Martin Luther's intentions fairly and even whether this was what he wanted. One has to keep in mind that Baeck was not really interested in Luther himself or in the historical situation facing Luther when he developed his ideas. Luther appears as merely a part of the dispute with Christianity in the post-Enlightenment environment, when historico-critical questioning shattered the basis of Bible and tradition as well as the old concept of a Christian occident.

Therefore, this representation of Christianity is more a sign of deliberate and schematic polemics than the attempt to give the opposing view due credit through differentiated presentation.[89] Elucidating the contrast between Judaism and Christianity by ascribing them respectively, as classical or romantic religion is typical: Baeck obviously uses contemporary German philosophical schemes.

Any objective analysis cannot avoid the insight that Baeck's polarized model of mystery and commandment probably works much better within the traditions of one single faith than in the comparison of two different ones. Baeck's polarizing

---

[86] Kant. *Metaphysik der Sitten*, Tugendlehre, Einleitung XII b.

[87] Kant, *Kritik der praktischen Vernunft,* 1. Teil, 1. Buch, 1. Hauptstück, § 7 and ibid., 1. Teil, 1. Hauptstück, § 7, Anmerkung.

[88] Kant, *Kritik der praktischen Vernunft,* 1. Teil, 1. Buch, 1. Hauptstück, § 1, also ibid., 1. Teil, 1. Buch, 1. Hauptstück, § 7; also *Grundlegung zur Metaphysik der Sitten*, 1. und 2. Abschnitt.

[89] On Baeck's limited approach to Christianity see Reinhold Mayer. *Christentum und Judentum in der Schau Leo Baecks*. Studia Delitzschiana, 6. Stuttgart, 1961, pp. 44–9.

construction makes it difficult to fairly evaluate the developments and schools of thought in Christianity as well as Judaism. There is room to argue whether or not this was Baeck's intention. There seem to be clear indications of an intended and conscious one-sidedness of ideas and positions for the sake of apologetics and critique.[90] The separation of influences on the church – the Jewish-biblical tradition on the one side and Hellenistic influences on the other – appears to be especially questionable. Baeck's equation: "Gnosticism is Christianity without Judaism and, in that sense, pure Christianity"[91] is openly polemical. The church may not always have liked the various influences united in its tradition. Yet however devastating Christian scholarly judgment might have been, its inheritance from Judaism was rarely disputed and was even acknowledged as its root by Paul.[92] Baeck's theory of "Judaism in the Church" becomes even more problematic when he tries to distil this Jewish foundation from Christianity in order to create an "objective" image of it.

Baeck's attempts to include Jesus and the Gospels in this Jewish foundation are also striking, yet highly questionable as further examination of the history of Christian theology in order to extract Jewish influences on the one hand and genuine Christian (i.e. non-Jewish) influences on the other. Baeck defines two paths in the Christian history of religion, namely, a Jewish one reaching from Jesus via Pelagius and Duns Scotus to Calvin, and a Christian one starting with Paul and leading to Augustine and Luther. However, any proper perception of Christianity must understand it as a mix of various influences, just as Judaism is. Baeck's course division suggests that he was less interested in the theological questions of his time than in presenting a highly stylized view of Christianity and Judaism.

But what was Baeck's motivation for simplification on one side and for extraction of a "Jewish strand" from within Christian theology on the other? If we consider the discussion with Harnack, we might see Baeck's motivation: he turned against an early historical Bible criticism that was not very concerned whether or not to eliminate text passages in the Old Testament that seemed to be "unchristian." And Baeck opposed Christian ignorance, which despicably rejects of Judaism by deeming it a faith of the past, and declares Christianity to be the "absolute religion." Baeck issues the explicit polemical warning[93] not to underestimate the vitality and freshness of the Jewish faith.

---

[90] Mayer, *Christentum und Judentum*, pp. 48–9.
[91] Baeck, *Romantic Religion*, p. 250.
[92] Rom. 11:18.
[93] Walter Jacob entitled his essay on Leo Baeck "Modern Polemic." In his view, Baeck represents *the* contemporary prototype of this genre. Walter Jacob. *Christianity through Jewish Eyes: The Quest for Common Ground*. Cincinnati: 1974, pp. 137–161, notes: pp. 261–263.

Leo Baeck and Martin Luther in Conflict

Baeck's polemic emerges from two analytical methods: first, everything he values in Christianity is carefully extracted and then attributed to Judaism.[94] In this way, Jesus and the Gospel, as opposed to Paul, can suddenly end up in the "Jewish camp." Baeck uses this principle all the way through when dealing with the Church tradition. It culminates in the development of his polarized model: the Pauline-romantic and the Jewish-classical religion. At this point, the portrayal of Judaism as well as Christianity becomes ahistorical, with Baeck fully accepting this.

On the other hand, parallel phenomena in both religions are viewed positively in Judaism and negatively in Christianity. For example, grace in Judaism joins happily with the positive term of commandment. In Christian terms, however, grace becomes the very epitome of passivity and egocentricity.

All this makes the conclusion likely that Baeck had only limited access to the complex and perhaps somewhat unsystematic world of Luther's thinking. And we also have reason to believe that a thorough understanding was not at the center of his endeavor. Nevertheless, Baeck recognized the key points of Luther's teaching.

Leo Baeck: A Founding Father of Jewish-Christian Dialogue

Baeck had a special relationship to the Jewish-Christian dialogue throughout his life. In a certain sense, he was its spiritual precursor.

To Baeck, Jewish-Christian cooperation meant mutual respect of the differences and not an empty, meaningless balancing out of the centuries of sacred traditions. Yet the mild-mannered man, so often open to compromise, nevertheless had no patience with attempts at defamation or misrepresentation of his faith.

On the other hand, his portrayal of Christianity was not always free of theoretical construction and displayed no lack of polemic.

He viewed the Church as the successor to ancient Greco-Roman civilization, characterized by its ideal of beauty and harmony. Everything there was designed to be perfect, complete and in tune with each other. Whether in Greek art or in philosophy, the perfection and the balance of things right up to the harmony of the kingdoms is its most compelling characteristic.

---

[94] Mayer, *Christentum und Judentum*, p. 87.

This civilization lacked a dynamic element, however, a restlessness and dissatisfaction with the world as it is. The forward-pressing messianic moment, the prophetic protest against the imperfection and unjust order of the world was absent.

For this reason, a hideous contempt for humanity, brutality, terror and slavery could exist in Greece and Rome, side by side with the admirable achievements of beauty, the mind, technology and culture. This was not considered as contradictory and posed no serious problem. Prophetic criticism was absent, as well as a sense of ethical absoluteness, of the sanctity of each human life, and beyond that, of nature in general. An Amos, an Isaiah or a Jeremiah could not have existed there.

Baeck is most critical of Lutheranism. The "Doctrine of the two Kingdoms", which divided the sphere of human beings into that which belonged to the State and that which belonged to God, is here taken to an extreme. In Baeck's account, the Lutheran Church abdicated all responsibility for the worldly state of the people and left it to State authorities. Morality became so removed from religion that individuals seemed to be guaranteed a clear conscience concerning worldly affairs. What did matters of the world have to do with the individual anyway?

These tendencies led in Baeck's view to an authoritarian state and the silent acceptance of National Socialism by many. A police state allowing no room for individual decisions developed directly from Lutheranism, Baeck admonishes. The Nazi State was the logical consequence of such a misguided theological evolution.

On the other hand, Baeck was one of the Jewish intellectuals who enthusiastically supported the "reclaiming of Jesus" into Judaism. In 1938, at the height of National Socialism, he published his book on the Gospel as a document of the history of the Jewish faith, *"Das Evangelium als Urkunde der jüdischen Glaubensgeschichte."* He showed that Jesus led his entire life as an exemplary Jew who would never have considered founding a new religion, not to speak of being worshipped as God. Baeck described Jesus as follows:

> We see a man [...] before us whose entire being demonstrates Jewish character, every aspect so clearly and characteristically revealing the purity and goodness of Judaism; he was a man who, such as he was, could only have developed out of the firm roots of Judaism, and he could only win over his students and followers, such as they were, out of these roots; he was a man who could move through his life and to his death only here, in this Jewish realm – a Jew among Jews.[95]

---

[95] Albert H. Friedlander. *Leo Baeck*, p. 123: "Einen Mann sehen wir [...] vor uns, der in allen den Linien und Zeichen seines Wesens das jüdische Gepräge aufzeigt, in ihnen so eigen und so klar das Reine und Gute des Judentums offenbart, einen Mann, der als der, welcher er war, nur aus dem Boden des Judentums hervorwachsen konnte und nur aus diesem Boden hervor seine Schüler und Anhänger, so wie sie waren, erwerben

Baeck described the cornerstones of a true Jewish-Christian dialogue in his lecture on "Judaism, Christianity, and Islam" as:

[...] the knowledge and the acceptance of the differences and similarities of religions; in order to understand those, one has to be aware of one's own religious identity. In this sense, his contribution to the development of Jewish-Christian understanding cannot be overestimated.[96]

It is this insight in the value of identity that can serve as an important inheritance for today.

---

konnte, einen Mann, der hier allein, in diesem jüdischen Bereiche [...] durch sein Leben und in seinen Tod gehen konnte – ein Jude unter Juden."

[96] Leo Baeck. *Judentum, Christentum und Islam.* Rede gehalten von Ehren-Großpräsident Dr. Leo Baeck anlässlich der Studientagung der Districts-Loge Kontinental-Europa XIX in Bruxelles, 22. April 1956.

Dalia Marx

Liturgy Composed on the Brink of Catastrophe – Examination of "Akdamut Millin" by R. Meir from Worms (late 11th century) and R. Leo Baeck's Hirtenbrief for Kol Nidre Service (1935)[1]

This paper is dedicated to Yente and Joel Lieberman, my great-grandparents, who lived in Düsseldorf and perished in Theresienstadt.

Through out the ages, in times of joy and in sorrow, Jews have lifted their eyes to the Almighty with passion, anticipation and hope. The language and medium that they used was that of prayer. Jacob Petuchowski, the renowned scholar of Jewish liturgy, has described the *Siddur*, the Jewish prayer book, as the diary of the Jewish people – the laughter and tears of dozens of generations have been inscribed on it and soaked in it. The slavery of Egypt and the subsequent Exodus, the Jerusalem Temple in its splendor and its destruction, the trials and tribulations of exile, plagues and persecutions – they are all embedded and given voice in the liturgy.[2]

Prayers, liturgical hymns or poems, the so-called *piyyutim*, and ritual customs that reflect Jewish experience throughout the generations, make the events that initiated them, vivid and present in the lives of those who pray and those who appreciate the liturgy.

Event-oriented Prayers

Obviously, most of the words of prayer that were spoken by Jewish men, women and children throughout the ages did not find their way into the standardized prayer book. Most of them are lost, some are recorded in books, private diaries and journals but are rarely given resonance in prevalent practice.

This type of prayer, written in response to specific events or for special occasions, may be called event-oriented or event-specific prayers. This type of liturgi-

---

[1] I would like to warmly thank Professor Shulamit Elizur, Professor Avigdor Sinan, Dr. David Levine and Dr. Daniel Stoekl Ben Ezra for their helpful comments and suggestions

[2] Jakob J. Petuchowski. *Prayerbook Reform in Europe. The Liturgy of European Liberal and Reform Judaism.* New York: World Union for Progressive Judaism, 1968, pp. 22–23.

cal composition addressing certain events resembles ephemeral literature, such as journalism. What is acute and meaningful today, will probably have little meaning, even in the near future.[3]

Paradoxically, what may help in preserving some event-specific prayers and what may keep them relevant over time, is a lack of particular attributes and context. The more the language is generalized, the more the formulation transcends time-dependent circumstances and people will be able to find meaning in it for generations to come. I hope to demonstrate this liturgical rule today.

I would like to add one other presupposition before we turn to the texts. Liturgy can not only be dealt in textual terms. Liturgy is a complex human phenomenon that reflects theology, sociology, psychology, politics, history and more and should be treated as such. Prayer is one of the most important forms of expression for religious people, people who contemplate the world through religious eyes and Judaism is clearly a liturgical religion.[4]

Our goal here is twofold: to appreciate the liturgist craftsmanship, the poetical and literary qualities of the text but also to try and look beyond the text, to explore the intent of the composer, the ways in which the text was perceived and the extant and forms in which it was preserved.

The Liturgical Pieces that Will Be Dealt with Here

Today I would like to discuss two texts that may be categorized as event-oriented liturgies. Both are not "prayers" in the strict sense of the word, since neither of them addresses God in a direct way. The two texts are very different from each other and at the same time have quite some common denominators that make an exploration of their similarities worthwhile. Let me express the hope that we will never again have a need or occasion to compose texts like these.

The first piece we will present is a *piyyut*, called *Akdamut Millin*, a liturgical hymn written by Rabbi Meir son of Rabbi Yitzhak, a cantor in the Jewish community of Worms who lived in the late eleventh century. The *piyyut* was composed shortly before the first crusade and the massacre of the Rhine valley Jewish communities in 1096,[5] known in Jewish tradition as גזירות תתנ"ו, *Gezerot Tatnu* – the

---

[3] For example, the prayers that were composed in the context of Israel's disengagement from Gaza in the summer of 2005 (from the right and from the left poles of the political map), however powerful in their moment, seem to lose their impact only a few months after the events. An article I wrote about this liturgical phenomenon will be published in Hebrew in winter 2006.

[4] Petuchowski, pp. 22–23.

[5] We can not date *Akdamut* with precision. According to Sheshar, Yahalom and Sokolof it was composed in close proximity to the massacres of 1096 (see footnote 26).

decrees of the year 4856.[6] *Akdamut* is intended to be recited, or actually sung, in the Torah reading service on the festival of *Shavuot*.[7]

According to post-biblical Jewish tradition, Torah was given to Moses at Sinai on this day, the fiftieth day after Passover. I'd like to suggest that in this poetical piece, though in a rather subtle manner, the fears of the German Jewish communities are embedded and I will try to show that the *piyyut* addresses these concerns in an indirect manner.

The second text was written eight hundred and thirty years later in the same geographical territory that is today's Germany. It is a "pastoral letter," a "Hirtenbrief", addressing the congregation, written by Rabbi Leo Baeck, in honor of whom we are gathered here today.

Baeck, the head of the Reichsvertretung der Juden in Deutschland (Reich Deputation of German Jews), wrote this piece in Berlin in the fall of 1935, just a few weeks after the legislation of the Nuremberg laws, laws that deprived German Jews of legal rights and of their status as citizens. Baeck sent this address to all Jewish congregations in Germany.

It was to be read before the *Kol Nidre*, the service commencing the *Yom Kippur* that year. It is important to note, that the Nazi authorities did not object to Jewish gatherings in synagogues for purpose of prayer until the Kristallnacht in 1938. These were the only gatherings that did not require special permission. However, when the Gestapo heard of this text, they prohibited its public recitation, for reasons that we will examine in a moment, and forced the Reichsvertretung to send telegrams to all congregations ensuring that it was not to be read.[8]

Almost a millennium separates these two liturgical texts from each other. They differ in several ways: While Leo Baeck's address uses the vernacular of the community – German, *Akdamut* was written in Aramaic, a language known only to the more educated members of the Jewish community.

---

[6] See Robert Chazan. *European Jewry and the First Crusade*. Berkeley: University of California Press, 1987; Benjamin Kedar. *Crusade Historians and the Massacres of 1096*. In: *Jewish History*, 12, 1998, pp. 11–31; Jonathan Riley Smith. *The First Crusade and the Persecution of the Jews*. In: *Studies in Church History*, 21, 1984, pp. 51–72; *Yehudim mul ha-tselav. Gezerot ttn"v be-historyah uve-historyografyah*. Yerushalayim: Magnes, 2000.

[7] In his book *Sefer ha-gezerot ashkenaz ve-tsarfat*, published just a few months after the end of the Second World War in 1945, Abraham Meir Habermann makes a direct comparison between the pogroms in the German and French communities in the Middle Ages and the horrors of the holocaust. He states that while it is too painful for people in his time to deal with the Shoah and the devastation it caused, it is important to deal with the persecutions of the Jews in medieval Europe (p. 11). According to my knowledge, he was the first one to draw this comparison in a scholarly publication.

[8] Leonard Baker. *Days of Sorrow and Pain. Leo Baeck and the Berlin Jews*. New York: Macmillan, 1978, pp. 203–204.

While we know a great deal about the context of the composition of Baeck's address, we know very little about the circumstances in which *Akdamut* was composed. According to some testimonies, R. Meir of Worms, the composer of *Akdamut*, died shortly before the first crusade and his son, Isaac, was actually murdered in 1096.[9]

The texts also differ in their reception in subsequent Jewish tradition. *Akdamut* is still read every year on *Shavuot* in all synagogues following European tradition,[10] and is one of the liturgical highlights of the day.[11] Baeck's text is mentioned sometimes in rabbinic sermons and study sessions, but has not entered the prayer book and is rarely used in any liturgical context.

While *Akdamut* represents the ongoing tribulations of the Jewish life in exile, Leo Baeck's Hirtenbrief embodies the sudden insult and vulnerability of the German Jews of his time. The texts differ in their liturgical context, their literary qualities and genre and their theological message.

This said, it is interesting to note the similarities the two texts share. These similarities are prominent enough to make a typological examination interesting, insightful and instructive. Let me briefly list six of them:

- Both texts were composed by central rabbinic figures who served as prominent leaders of their respective Jewish communities.
- Both texts were meant to be recited at crucial moments in well attended services on two of the most important holidays of the Jewish calendar – *Yom Kippur* and *Shavuot*.
- Both texts address the congregation in a direct and explicit manner.
- Both texts were written in times of troubles. Both seem to deal, as I would like to propose, with the current hardships but also with upcoming difficulties and aim to prepare the hearts for it.[12]

---

[9] Grossman, Avraham. *Hakhme Ashkenaz ha-rishonim korotehem, darkam be-hanhagat ha-tsibur, yet-siratam ha-ruhanit. Me-reshit yishuvam ve-'ad li-gezerot 856 (1096)*. Yerushalayim: Magnes, 761 [2001], p. 292; Encyclopaedia Judaica, vol. 11. Jerusalem: Keter, col. 1255.

[10] *Akdamut* is performed in synagogues that follow both the Ashkenazi rite and the Chasidic rite, sometimes also called *"nusah sefarad"* or Sefarad rite. In the prayer books that follow the Spanish-Portuguese rite, one would find a different *piyyut* that is recited before the Torah reading in *Shavuot*. It is a poem by Israel Ben Moses Najara, called *Ketubbah*, where the Torah is compared to a marriage contract between God and Israel.

[11] The centrality of *Akdamut* is, among other things, derived from the fact that unlike the other two pilgrimage festivals (*Sukkot* and *Pesah*), *Shavuot* does not have distinctive and special religious commandments. In a way, *Akdamut*, read in the framework of the Torah service of *Shavuot*, is what gives the holiday its unique nature, and in the eyes of many is the liturgical highlight of the day.

[12] This argument is rather evident regarding Baeck's Hirtenbrief and somewhat tentative when it comes to *Akdamut*, as I would like to show.

- Neither attempts to gloss over contemporary plights. Neither has a theurgic intent, that is to say, none of them aims to justify the current hardships as punishments or heavenly retribution for Israel's sins.
- Both texts can be fully understood and be appreciated only from distant time, since the full scale of the catastrophe was not revealed until after they were composed and originally performed.

Comparing these liturgical texts may also grant us an insight, even if partial and tentative, to more general issues of Jewish liturgy, what its goals might be, and how to assess its function and action in the religious context, for which it was intended. Let us now examine the two liturgical compositions.

Akdamut Millin – a liturgical poem by R. Meir of Worms for Shavuot (late 11th century)

Akdamut has ninety lines. The first forty four lines begin with a double alphabetical acrostic. The first letters of the next forty six lines make up another acrostic which includes the author's name and his aspiration to be blessed with Torah and good deeds (מאיר biר רבי יצחק יגדל בתורה ובמעשים טובים אמן וחזק אמן ואמץ). Each line ends with the sound "-ta" which is a common grammatical suffix in Aramaic. But the word "ta" in Aramaic is also the imperative form of "ata" – "come." The repetition of that sound may therefore serve as an ongoing invitation to the listeners to come and to be part of the Torah and those people studying it. Here are the first eight lines of *Akdamut* that describe the human incapacity to praise God's majesty:

אַקְדָּמוּת מִילִין וְשָׁרָיוּת שׁוּתָא
אַוְלָא שָׁקִילְנָא הַרְמָן וּרְשׁוּתָא
בְּבָבֵי תְּרֵי וּתְלָת דְּאֶפְתַּח בְּנַקְשׁוּתָא
בְּבָרֵי דְבָרֵי וְטָרֵי עֲדֵי לְקַשְׁשׁוּתָא
גְּבוּרָן עָלְמִין לֵיהּ וְלָא סְפֵק פְּרִישׁוּתָא
גְּוִיל אִלּוּ רְקִיעֵי קְנֵי כָּל חוּרְשָׁתָא
דְּיוֹ אִלּוּ יַמֵּי וְכָל מֵי כְנִישׁוּתָא
דַּיְירֵי אַרְעָא סַפְרֵי וְרַשְׁמֵי רַשְׁוָתָא

As an introduction to the words and commencement of my speech
I begin by taking authorization and permission
In two and three sections I shall commence with trembling

To talk and converse the sanctity of the eternal one
He has eternal strength that could not be described
Even if the Heavens were parchment and the forests quills
If all the oceans were ink as well as every gathered water
If the earth's inhabitants were scribes and records of initials[13]

In this paper we can't explore the poetic qualities of this moving *piyyut*,[14] rather, we will say a few words about its content. It starts with the praise of God, Creator of the world, and then describes how the angles sing God's praise. Now it moves on to assert that however lofty the angels in heaven might be, the people of Israel are greater.

The composer now demonstrates this assertion: כנסת ישראל (the assembly or entirety of Israel) is courted, as if she were a beautiful maiden, by the nations of the world who say to her: "Who is your beloved, beautiful one, for whose sake do you perish in a lion's den." Note that the image of the nations is not violent nor intimidating, but rather sweet and seductive. The assembly of Israel responds with a lengthy speech, during which the redemption and all the good it entails is described. Material and spiritual wealth is promised to all – yet only in the days to come, when the righteous will be rewarded. It gives a vivid description of the feast that awaits the righteous (אריסטון לצדיקֵי) in this idealized future.

The *piyyut* ends by turning from this messianic picture to the people in the synagogue, who are actually listening to its recitation; they are the true addressees of these words, not the nations of the world:

זַכָּאִין כַּד שָׁמְעַתּוּן שְׁבַח דָּא שִׁירָתָא
קְבִיעִין כֵּן תֶּהֱווֹן בְּהָנְהוּ חֲבוּרָתָא
וְתִזְכּוּן דִּי תֵיתְבוּן בְּעֵילָא דָרְתָא
אֲרֵי תְצִיתוּן לְמִילֵי דְנָפְקִין בְּהַדְרָתָא
מְרוֹמָם הוּא אֱלָהִין בְּקַדְמָא וּבַתְרַיְתָא
צְבִי וְאִתְרְעִי בָן וּמְסַר לָן אוֹרַיְתָא.[15]

---

[13] With minor changes the translation is based on the one in *Siddur Ahavat Shalom. The Complete Artscroll Siddur (Ashkenaz)*. New York: Artscroll, 2000, pp. 714–719.

[14] Yisakhar Ya'akovson. *Netiv binah*. Tel Aviv: Sinai, 1989, pp. 105–133. Unfortunately, I'm not aware of any non-Hebrew commentary to *Akdamut*.

[15] At this point the scriptural reading for *Shavuot*, Exodus 19–20:23, is read where the Ten Commandments appear. The initial costume was to recite *Akdamut* after reading the first verse of the Torah portion. What may explain this odd practice is *Akdamut*'s original liturgical function; it was a poetic introduction to the Aramaic translation of the scriptures, since until sometime in the Middle Ages the Torah was translated to Aramaic verse by verse. The reading of the translation would begin then, after the reading of the first verse. And this

O righteous ones just as you heard the praise in this song
So may you be appointed among that company
Being privileged to be seated in the foremost row
If you listened to His words that emanate in majesty
God is exalted in the beginning and when all is done
He desired and selected us and He gave us the Torah.

In this statement we may find an unspoken message – times are not easy and danger might be near but you all should remain strong in your faith. Those faithful, will gain good reward.

R. Baeck's Hirtenbrief – A Liturgical Address for Kol Nidre at Yom Kippur, (1935)

First, let us see the text of Baeck's address:[16]

In dieser Stunde steht ganz Israel vor seinem Gotte, dem richtenden und vergebenden. Vor ihm wollen wir allesamt unseren Weg prüfen, prüfen, was wir getan und was wir unterlassen, prüfen, wohin wir gegangen und wovon wir ferngeblieben sind. Wo immer wir gefehlt haben, wollen wir offen bekennen, wir haben gesündigt und wir wollen mit dem festen Willen zur Umkehr vor Gott beten: Vergib uns.

Wir stehen vor unserem Gotte. Mit derselben Kraft, mit der wir unsere Sünden bekannt, die Sünden der Einzelnen und die der Gesamtheit, sprechen wir es mit dem Gefühl des Abscheus aus, dass wir die Lüge, die sich gegen uns wendet, die Verleumdung, die sich gegen unsere Religion und ihre Zeugnisse kehrt, tief unter unseren Füssen sehen. Wir bekennen uns zu unserem Glauben und zu unserer Zukunft. – Wer hat der Welt das Geheimnis des Ewigen, des einen Gottes gekündet? Wer hat der Welt den Sinn für die Reinheit der Lebensführung, der Reinheit der Familie geoffenbart? Wer hat der Welt die Achtung vor dem Menschen, dem Ebenbild Gottes gegeben? Wer hat der Welt das Gebot der Gerechtigkeit, den sozialen Gedanken gewiesen? Der Geist der Propheten Israels, die Offenbarung Gottes an das jüdische Volk hat in dem

---

is why *Akdamut*, which was composed in Aramaic and serves as a prelude to the scripture translation, would be inserted at that point. Later, when the scriptures were no longer translated (see: *Tur, Orah Hayim* 145), the reading of the *piyyut*, in a manner that interrupted the Torah reading was no longer acceptable. And due to rabbinic objections, *Akdamut*'s recitation has been done right before the scriptures were read. See Ya'akovson, pp. 99–105.

[16] Leo Baeck. *Ansprache zum Kol Nidre des Versöhnungstages 6. Oktober 1935.* In: Ernst A. Simon. *Aufbau im Untergang. Jüdische Erwachsenenbildung im nationalsozialistischen Deutschland als geistiger Widerstand.* Tübingen: Mohr, 1959, pp. 39–41. There are some other versions of this prayer. One of them can be found in: Eric H. Boehm. *We Survived. Fourteen Histories of the Hidden and Hunted of Nazi Germany.* Santa Barbara: Clio Press, 1966, p. 285. However, the text cited above is what Berenbaum claims to be the original copy that came out of Baeck's typewriter. See Michael Berenbaum. *A Promise to Remember. The Holocaust in the Words and Voices of its Survivors.* Boston: Bulfinch Press, 2003.

allen gewirkt. In unserem Judentum ist es erwachsen und wächst es. An diesen Tatsachen prallt jede Beschimpfung ab.

Wir stehen vor unserem Gott; auf Ihn bauen wir. In Ihm hat unsere Geschichte, hat unser Ausharren in allem Wandel, unsere Standhaftigkeit in aller Bedrängnis ihre Wahrheit und ihre Ehre. Unsere Geschichte ist eine Geschichte seelischer Größe, seelischer Würde. Sie fragen wir, wenn sich Angriff und Kränkung gegen uns kehren, wenn Not und Leid uns umdrängen. Von Geschlecht zu Geschlecht hat Gott unsere Väter geführt. Er wird auch uns und unsere Kinder durch unsere Tage hindurch leiten.

Wir stehen vor unserem Gott. Sein Gebot, das wir erfüllen, gibt uns Kraft. Ihm beugen wir uns, und wir sind aufrecht vor den Menschen. Ihm dienen wir, und wir bleiben fest in allem Wechsel des Geschehens, demütig vertrauen wir auf Ihn, und unsere Bahn liegt deutlich vor uns, wir sehen unsere Zukunft.

Ganz Israel steht in dieser Stunde vor seinem Gotte. Unser Gebet, unser Vertrauen, unser Bekennen ist das aller Juden auf Erden. Wir blicken aufeinander und wissen von uns, und wir blicken zu unserem Gotte empor und wissen von dem, was bleibt.
'Siehe, nicht schläft und nicht schlummert Er, der Israel hütet. Er, der Frieden schafft in seinen Höhen, wird Frieden schaffen über uns und ganz Israel.'

Trauer und Schmerz erfüllen uns. Schweigend, durch Augenblicke des Schweigens vor unserem Gotte, wollen wir dem, was unsere Seele erfüllt, Ausdruck geben. Eindringlicher als alle Worte es vermöchten, wird diese schweigende Andacht sprechen.

In this hour the whole house of Israel stands before its Got, the God of justice and mercy. We shall all examine our path before Him. We shall examine what we have done and what we have failed to do. We shall examine where we have gone and where we have failed to go. Wherever we have sinned, we will confess it freely. We will say: 'we have sinned' and, with fervent resolve to repent before God, we will pray that God may forgive us.

We stand before our God. With the same strength with which we have acknowledged our sins of the community, we shall express our abhorrence of the lie directed against us and of the slander of our faith and its expressions. This slander is far beneath us. We believe in our faith and our future. Who proclaimed the secrets of the eternal and the one and only God to the world? Who revealed to the world an understanding for a life of purity, for the purity of the family? Who brought the world respect for Man made in the image of God? Who brought the world the commandment of justice, of social thought? The spirit of the prophets of Israel. The revelation of God to the Jewish people had a part in all of these. It sprang from our existence as Jews and continues to grow there. Any insult will fall away when it is cast against these facts.

We stand before our God. Our strength is in Him. It is in Him that our history finds its truth and honor. He is the source of our survival through every chance, of our fortitude in all our trials. Our history is the history of spiritual greatness, spiritual dignity. We turn to it when attack and insult are directed against us, when need and suffering press upon us. God led our fathers from generation to generation. He will continue to lead us and our children through our days.

We stand before our God. His commandments that we fulfill give us the strength so that we bow before him and stand straight before other men. We serve him and we remain steadfast in all the challenges and the happenings of the world. Humbly, we place our trust in him, and our path lies clearly before us and we see our future.

In this hour, all of Israel stands before its God and our prayer, our trust, and our affirmation of our faith is that of all Jews on this earth. We look at each other, and we know each other with profound knowledge, and we look up to our God and we know what is and will remain.

'Look ye, the shepherd of Israel, He does not sleep nor does He slumber [Psalm 121, 4]. He who creates peace in the heavens shall create peace for us and all of Israel [citation from the Kaddish].'

Mourning and pain fills our hearts. Through moments of silence before our God, we want to give expression to that which fills our souls. More forcefully than any words could ever do, this silent prayer will speak.[17]

R. Baeck uses the momentous occasion of the holiest day in the Jewish calendar, the Day of Atonement, to invite the congregation for personal and communal reflection חשבון נפש, urging them to confess their sins. He reminds his addressees that "In this hour the whole house of Israel stands before its God" – they are not alone, all people of Israel stand in this awesome time for celestial judgment.

Nevertheless, this is not a normal rabbinic address for the Day of Atonement, Baeck clarifies, though in an implicit manner, that their current distressing state is not the act of the almighty and should not be perceived as a punishment from him. In fearless words he states:

With the same strength with which we have acknowledged our sins of the community, we shall express our abhorrence of the lie directed against us and of the slander of our faith and its expressions.

Addressing the people in the synagogue as well as those who are the source of the "lies", he mentions the contributions that Judaism brought to the world: the faith in one eternal God, the respect for human being created in the image of God, social justice and more.

Again and again Baeck stresses that in God we trust and in front of Him we stand together affirming our faith. He concludes his Hirtenbrief saying: "More forcefully than any words could ever do, this silent prayer will speak."

No words may encapsulate the sadness, the fear and the rage of the German Jews, gathered in the holiest day of the year, just a few weeks after the legislation

---

[17] This translation is taken from Michael Berenbaum.

of the Nuremberg Laws.[18] He is neither trying to sooth his congregants nor to promise them that the clouds gathering over Europe will go away.[19]

As mentioned above, R. Baeck's prayer was prohibited to be read publicly. We do not know how many synagogues recited the prayer in spite of the Nazi instructions. The historian Leonard Backer assumes that: "many did, so many that it was almost a collective act of defiance on the part of the German rabbinate."[20] Baeck himself was arrested shortly after and was kept in Gestapo facilities. He was released after a short time and no charges were brought against him.[21]

This prayer is both German and Jewish. Baker writes: "Scholars have dissected it to show how Leo Baeck's German-Jewish culture influenced its shape, its organization, its wording." However, says Baker, above all: "This is a human prayer, a statement of the individual of his rights to hold beliefs, of his pride and of his dignity."[22]

While we should accept Baker's account, that Leo Baeck is defining the ultimate condition of humanity, we need also to remember his role as rabbinic authority and communal leader, and realize how this fact had an impact on his listeners and addressees. This Jewish community was severely offended and insulted by the recent legislation that deprived them of their status as German citizens. Puzzled and frightened they gazed at the darkening skies of their homeland, seeking words of guidance.

Common and Different Features of the Texts

Let us now see what can be learnt from the juxtaposition of these two liturgical texts.

It is important to begin by mentioning the fundamental difference between the texts. *Akdamut* reflects the ongoing experience of exile, alongside with what one may subsequently see as a premonition of an upcoming catastrophe; whereas Leo Baeck's text is informed by an acute awareness of crisis and consciously desires

---

[18] Some report, that Baeck was saying already in 1933 that the thousand year old history of the Jews in Germany was at an end. *Li'o Bek. Manhigut ve-haghut 1933–1945*. Avraham Barkay (ed.). Yerushalayim: Merkaz Zalman Shazar le-toldot Yisra'el, 2000.

[19] A description of Baeck reading the Hirtenbrief in the Fasanenstraße Synagogue on *Yom Kippur* 1935 can be found in: Anne E. Neimark. *One Man's Valor. Leo Baeck and the Holocaust*. New York: Dutton, 1986, pp. 41–44.

[20] Baker, p. 206.

[21] The Gestapo continued its harassment by arresting Dr. Otto Hirsch, another leading figure in the Reichsvertretung. Baeck related to the occurrences that let to his and Dr. Hirsch's arrestment in an interview he gave in the fifties. The bulk of the story appears in Baker, pp. 204–208.

[22] Baker, p. 206.

to give it expression. The *piyyut* addresses an unfortunate but precedent situation in exile, while what is particularly heart-rending about Leo Baeck's Hirtenbrief is the presence of insult and indignation on the part of community who saw itself as an integral part of German society and culture.

This might assist us in explaining why *Akdamut*'s idiom is generalized, its language directed towards the Jewish experience of exile as a whole. Sadly enough, Jews could identify with the lady who is being threatened by the lions in many times throughout the history. This also will serve to explain the acceptance of *Akdamut* into the standard holiday prayerbook.

On the other hand, Baeck's piece might be too event-specific and associated too strongly with the trauma of the upcoming Holocaust, and therefore not be able to capture ongoing Jewish existential sentiment in its liturgical formulation. That said, the power and eloquence of Baeck's meditation was translated into several languages[23] and has been cause for reference and quotation by preachers and teachers over the last decades.

Let us now compare some more aspects of the two texts:

Author: In both cases, we see a single leader standing in front of his bewildered congregation, trying to strengthen its members in time of hardship. We should consider the texts as well as their performance as acts of leadership.

Existential context: In both cases the texts are written in order to address well established, highly educated and self assured Jewish communities, which for several generations knew relative serenity. In both cases, the tranquillity was or was about to be interrupted.[24] And in both cases, the current troubles were just a prelude to trials that were much more devastating.

---

[23] There are no less than three Hebrew translations of the Hirtenbrief that are known to me: *Ha-Shoah be-ti'ud. Mivhar te'udot 'al hurban yehude germanyah, polin u-Verit ha-Mo'atsot*. Yitshak Arad, Yisrael Gutman Abraham Margaliot (ed.). Yerushalayim, 1978, pp. 81–82; Akibah Ernst Simon. *Pirke hayim. Binyan tokh hurban*. Tel Aviv: Sifriyat po'alim, 1987, 119–120. Akibah Ernst Simon in Barkay, *Li'o Bek*, pp. 53–53.

[24] Even though *Akdamut* is couched in a general idiom, there is an indication of the authors contextualizing intent. Joseph Yahalom and Michael Sokolof indicate in the article *Minhagan shel Yisra'el Torah hi' [...] leshorer shir ha-kadosh ha-zeh,* published in Haaretz (May 25th, 2004), that *Akdamut* took the place of an older *piyyut* that served as an introduction to the Torah reading and translation for *Shavuot* (see also the on-line edition of Haaretz http://new.haaretz.co.il/hasite/pages/ShArtPE.jhtml?itemNo=431372&contrassID =2&subContrassID=5&sbSubContrassID=0, 31.10.2006). That hymn, called *Arkin Mosheh*, depicts a celestial drama, where the angles are struggling against the entrance of a human being (Moses) into the Divine shrine to take the stone tablets. God stands on the side of the stranger and dresses him with a glorious robe and grants him the rays of splendor with which he may fight the angles (see Joseph Heinemann. *Seridim me-yet-siratam ha-piyutit shel ha-meturgamenim ha-kodmim*. In: *Ha-Sifrut*, IV, 2, 1973, pp. 363–364. R. Meir knew this *piyyut*, but in his times, Yahalom and Sokolof say, it wasn't the struggle between heavenly creatures and humans but the ongoing struggle between them and the Christian surrounding that troubled the minds of the

Medium: In both texts the author chooses to address the congregation through liturgical means and in a liturgical context, not only making use of a dramatic moment during a central holiday, when many people gather in the house of God, but also by the main theme of the holiday: the Torah and the people studying and cherishing it in the case of *Akdamut* that is read in *Shavuot*; confession and soul searching in Baeck's text that was composed for the Day of Atonement.

Addressees: Unlike R. Meir, who wrote his piece in Aramaic, the rabbinic language of the scholarly class of the Jews, R. Baeck's address is written in the vernacular. The language of *Akdamut* was not a spoken one at the time of its composition, it was written in a rather artificial Aramaic and it was understood only by few, even in the synagogue itself,[25] while Baeck's Hirtenbrief is intended for all ears – Jews and non-Jews, persecuted, persecutors as well as side-observers, Jews and non-Jewish leaders outside of the Third Reich alike. The text swiftly found its way to the United States.[26]

The role of Israel: Both texts emphasize the special role of Israel and the fact that the current difficulties do not change the unique bond between Israel and their Father in Heaven. But while *Akdamut* is a particularistic text and its author stresses the loyalty of the Jews to God, Baeck emphasizes the valuable contributions of the Jews to the world's culture.

Theology and rhetorical strategies: Both authors seek to address their communities but they do it using rather different methods. While *Akdamut* uses a narrated picturesque framework to demonstrate Israel's virtues, Leo Baeck uses theological terminology not only to demonstrate the merit of Israel itself but also its

---

Jews of Worms. Their poor state was perceived as proof for the mistaken ways of the Jews and the final victory of Ecclesia over Synagoga. This is the ground, they state, for the composition of *Akdamut* as the opening *piyyut* for the scriptural reading of the Holiday, in which we read: 'Now if you obey Me and keep My covenant, you shall be My special treasure [*segulah*] among all nations [...] You will be a kingdom of priests and a holy nation to me" (Leviticus 19:5–6). See also: *Madu'a hover piyut 'ha-Akdamut' be-aramit?* In: *Shanah be-Shanah*, 1984, p. 352.

[25] We will have to admit that the reason that *Akdamut* touches the hearts so profoundly is hardly its theology or its wording but rather the magnificent setting and its moving music, sang responsively by the cantor and the congregation. Deshen wrote that in many cases the latent or the symbolic aspects of the liturgy are much more meaningful to the participants than the actual wording and theological meaning. He demonstrates his thesis examining *Kol Nidre*, a dry legal formula, that has become one of the most attended services in the Jewish year cycle because of its time, its setting and its music (Shlomo Deshen. *The Kol Nidre Enigma. An Anthropological View of the Day of Atonement Liturgy. In: Ethnology*, vol. 18, 2, 1979, pp. 121–133). Sometimes it is the mysterious and cryptic nature of the liturgy that gives it its prestige. Regarding its musical qualities, we know that it was sung in earlier times, but we can't be sure that the melody that is used in contemporary synagogues is the "original" one. Professor Eliyahu Schleifer, from Hebrew Union College in Jerusalem, told me that the character and the psalmodic form of the tune, we use nowadays, are probably medieval.

[26] Baker, pp. 207–208.

contributions to the world and the culture, the very culture that now denounces them. Baeck asks:

- Who proclaimed the secrets of the eternal and the one and only God to the world?
- Who revealed to the world an understanding for a life of purity, for the purity of the family?
- Who brought the world respect for Man made in the image of God?
- Who brought the world the commandment of justice, of social thought?

He encourages his addressees to fully reject the lies propagated against them and to put their trust in the almighty.

While both texts are aimed at strengthening the hearts and the faith, it seems that *Akdamut*, in its eschatological framework is geared mainly to reinforce the religious conviction while Baeck's text turns mainly to the broken hearts of the German Jews and aims to guide them in their plight.

Another interesting difference in the rhetorical strategy, employed in these texts, is that R. Meir promises in vivid colors the good reward of the faithful ones, while R. Baeck's text is explicitly not messianic. The hope in his piece is drawn out of the high moral character of Israel, and in the faith in God, "The Shepherd of Israel." His acknowledgment of God's Sovereignty is poignant for there is no promise of reward in the world or in the world to come. Being a liberal Rabbi, he does not use eschatological terminology.[27] He uses the language of faith and covenant.

Baeck's Hirtenbrief ends in a somber manner, in a way that resembles Aaron the priest witnessing the death of his two children (Leviticus 10:3) in silence:

Mourning and pain fills our hearts. Through moments of silence before our God, we want to give expression to that which fills our souls. More forcefully than any words could ever do, this silent prayer will speak.

Acceptance and retrospect: In both cases, the meaning of the text could only be fully appreciated with the unfolding of future events. The significance of these compositions is redefined once we are aware of the fact that they were indeed composed on the brink of catastrophe. In a way, this resembles the German ex-

---

[27] Jakob Josef Petuchowski. *Guide to the Prayer Book*. Cincinnati, 1967, pp. 54–55 (Edited and published for internal use).

pressionist painters, whose art anticipated or even, predicted, according to some critics, the horrors of the twentieth century.[28]

Given this definition, we may sense a prophetic aspect in both texts. But even if we are reluctant to claim that R. Meir and R. Baeck had a premonition or a presentiment of the looming imminence of larger catastrophe, we must assert that both acquired their full meaning in retrospect. That too helped in their subsequent preservation and circulation.

Summary

Two Jewish event-oriented liturgical pieces were examined here, both separately and in juxtaposition. Both texts were composed in times of hardship and on the verge of a larger scale catastrophe. These differ from one another and yet carry many similarities in a way that made the typological comparison instructive. This examination may serve also as a modest device to enhance our understanding of the functions of Jewish liturgy, both as reflecting the concerns of the time of its creation, as a prism of times past, and as an educating tool and a spiritually empowering device. It can supply those who read it (or pray it) a meaningful experience, even centuries after its composition and original performance.

It seems that a liturgical piece at its best is well grounded in a concrete existential context and at the same time, can move the hearts in a way that distance of place, time and existential context do not spoil their significance, but rather intensify it.

Let me end by repeating the wish that this type of text will remain a historical relic and never be used because of actual circumstances.

May our prayers be for peace and serenity, thanking the Almighty for our fortunate destiny!

---

[28] The prophetic sense is apparent also in the work of writers and poets. Take for example the poetry of the Jewish poet Uri Zvi Greenberg who has predicted the Holocaust and its horrors in a terrifying precision in his poetry, a decade before the war. See Dan Miron. *Akdamut le-Atsag*. Yerushalayim: Mosad Bialik, 2002, pp. 127–150.

Jonah Sievers

Particularism, the Other and the Question of the Burial of Non-Jewish Spouses in a Jewish Cemetery[1]

I would like to dedicate this paper to my teacher *Ha-Rav ha-Gaon* Rabbi John Rayner z"l. I do this not only because he was a great teacher, but also because the subject of this paper, essentially the question how to solve the tension between particularism and universalism, was always one close to his heart. Rabbi John Rayner was one of the few persons I know that "embodied" pluralism. Despite his insistence on intellectual integrity, he was also capable to reach pragmatic solutions.

There are not many halakhic questions I can think of, which make me feel apologetic. The reason for this uneasiness will become clear in a moment as we proceed with our discussion.

The question if it is permissible to bury non-Jews in a Jewish cemetery, is really a "question of grave concern"[2] as the conservative Rabbi Bergman titled his *teshuvah* on this question. According to the JPPPI the rate of interfaith marriages among German Jews is above 60 percent.[3] Given the demographics of the German Jewish community which is an aging community, this question will become even more pressing than in the past.

At the outset I like to point out that there is nothing inherently unethical if non-Jews are denied burial in a Jewish cemetery. The question however is to the justification of such a denial. Thus we can agree with Rabbi Abraham Schorr who wrote:

The separateness is not a matter of envy, for also the religions of the non-Jewish nations are different from one another and the non-Jews never resent the fact that Jews do not eat with them non-kosher food. But only if a non-Jew sees that, concerning a prohibition which is directed to an individual, a Jew transgress this a few times, but refuses to do this when dealing with him, the non-Jew will think this is only because of a hatred of his religion. This is a case of envy.[4]

---

[1] The Hebrew texts, if not otherwise stated, are translated into English by the author.

[2] Ben Zion Bergman. *A Matter of Grave Concern*. In: Rabbinical Assembly Committee on Jewish Law and Standards. *Responsa. 1991–2000*. New York: The Rabbinical Assembly, 2002, pp. 418–425.

[3] *The Jewish People Between Thriving and Decline. The Jewish People 2004*. Rami Tal (ed.). Jerusalem: Jewish People Policy Planning Institute, 2005, p. 12.

[4] As reported by Ovadia Yosef. *She'elot u-teshuvot Yabia' omer. 'Al 'arba'at helke ha-Sh"'A*. Jerusalem: Yeshivat Porat Yosef uve-siyua Mosad ha-Rav Kuk, 714, *Yoreh De'ah* §36, pp. 284f.

There is also no question that it was the established Jewish custom up to the 19th century to have separate cemeteries for the exclusive burial of Jews only.

There seems to be no archaeological evidence for the burial of non-Jews in Jewish cemeteries[5] and there seems to be also indications from rabbinic literature to the institution of separate burials. The most cited example is found in the Targum to Ruth 1:17:

> Naomi said: "We have [our own] cemeteries." Ruth answers: "There I want to be buried."[6]

The halakhic discussion essentially centers around three talmudic passages, namely Git. 61a and Sanh. 46a, 47a. We will begin with the discussion with the passage in *Gittin* which is also adduced by those Rabbis who are permissive. This well-known passage reads:

> The Rabbis teach in a Baraita: We provide support for the Gentile poor along with [עם] the Jewish poor, and we visit the gentile sick along with [עם] the Jewish sick, we bury the gentile dead along with [עם] the Jewish dead, because of the way of peace.

The question is what is the meaning of the word that connects the two parts of this sentence? There are several possibilities. First it could mean that one buries non-Jews in the same place with Jews, i.e. alongside them. But it could also be translated in the sense of "just as". And since the *Baraita* says we do all these things only because of good neighbourly relations, one might think that it is only when we are dealing with the burial of Jews and non-Jews at the same moment, we bury also non-Jews, because it might create enmity, if we would only bury the Jews. Such an interpretation might yield the conclusion, that if we find a dead non-Jew somewhere in the desert we are not under the obligation to bury him. The combination of the second and the third possibility is given by Rashi who points out that one buries non-Jews if they are found slain together with Jews.[7]

All traditional commentators on *Gittin* 61a share the implication that non-Jews are not to be buried in Jewish graves. The Rashba and the Ritba explain Rashi's position as follows: the only reason why Jews accomplish all those activities, enumerated in *Gittin* 61a, is that they want to avoid enmity among the gentile population. However, the Ritba among others dissents and writes:

---

[5] David Golinkin. *Kevurat nokhrim be-vet kevurot yehudi*. In: *Teshuvot va'ad ha-halakhah shel keneset ha-rabanim be-Yisra'el*. David Golinkin (ed.). Jerusalem, 1998, pp. 287–299, here p. 296.

[6] See also the remark of Golinkin, ibid.

[7] Rashi, ad loc.

[…] the [word] עם should be understood to mean that as one busies oneself with Jewish dead, thus one busies oneself with gentile dead, and this is explicitly stated in the Yerushalmi [6:9] [...] likewise this is also explicitly stated in the Tosefta.[8]

If we take a closer look at those two passages, it will become clear that the interpretation of the Ritba is the most likely one:

> In a city with a Jewish and a non-Jewish population, the parnasim collect charity from the Jews as well as from the non-Jews, because of the ways of peace. One supports the poor of the non-Jews together with [עם] the poor of the Jews, because of the ways of peace. One eulogizes and buries the dead of the non-Jews, because of the ways of peace. One comforts the mourners of the non-Jews, because of the ways of peace.
>
> Tosefta Git. 3:13–14

> It is taught: In a city with a Jewish and a non-Jewish population, one Jewish and non-Jewish official, who collect charity from the Jews and the non-Jews. One supports the poor of the non-Jews and the poor of the Jews, and one visits the sick of the non-Jews and the sick of the Jews, and one buries the dead of the non-Jews and the dead of the Jews, and one comforts the mourners of the non-Jews and the mourners of the Jews, and one provides for the wedding of the brides of the non-Jews and the brides of the Jews, because of the ways of peace.
>
> Yerushalmi Git. 5:9 (47c)

Both sources, i.e. the *Tosefta* and the *Yerushalmi*, mentioned by the Ritba support this reading, and the vast majority of commentators conclude that Jews are obligated to bury a non-Jew if there are no relatives.

Maimonides mentions this *halakhah* in two places, once in *Hilkhot Avel* 14:12:

> One buries the dead of the non-Jews and comforts their mourners and visits their sick because of the ways of peace.

In *Hilkhot Melakhim* 10:12 he is much more explicit:

> [...] even concerning a non-Jew our sages commanded us to visit their sick, and to bury their dead with Jewish dead, and to provide for their poor among the poor Jews, because of the ways of peace. For, behold it is written: 'The Eternal One is good to all, and his mercy is upon all His works' [Ps. 145:9] and it is said 'Her ways are always pleasant ways, and all her paths peaceful' [Prov. 3:17].

---

[8] Ritba, ad loc.

Therefore, according to Maimonides, burying also non-Jews is a commandment and not only a means to keep up good neighbourly relationships. The *Tur* and the *Shulhan Arukh* support Maimonides' opinion as stated in *Hilkhot Avel*.

One buries the dead of the non-Jews with Jewish dead and comforts their mourners, because of the ways of peace and Rashi's explanation is that we do not bury them in Jewish graves, but care about their burial like one cares about the burial of a Jew.   Tur, Yoreh Deah §367

One buries the dead of the non-Jews und comforts their mourners, because of the ways of peace.
Shulhan Arukh, Yoreh Deah §1

However, there are liberal Rabbis, among them Rabbi John Rayner, who think Rashi's assertion that we bury them לא בקברי ישראל which literally means "not in the grave of Jews", does not refer to a Jewish cemetery, but to a grave proper. Thus, they hold, it is not forbidden to bury them in a Jewish cemetery, but only to bury them in the same grave as a Jew.[9]

Against this it is argued that if the Talmud really meant that we bury non-Jews alongside Jews, it could have used the word אצל, "next to" which is used by the Talmud in this sense when it states in Sanh. 47a שאין קוברין רשע אצל צדיק.[10]

The assumption of all these interpretations is that the sources speak about the place of burial. But this must not necessarily be the case. Rabbi Golinkin convincingly explains that these passages speak about the financial aspect of all these activities. Actually the topic at the beginning of all three sources is the institutionalization of a charity system. All other activities have to be understood in this regard. If Golinkin's reading is correct, it follows that this passage is not relevant to our question at all.

In addition we might ask about the legal status of a Jewish cemetery. Rabbi Kohler has pointed out that the idea that the whole Jewish cemetery is consecrated even those places where there are no graves, is of late origin.[11] Thus we can understand why Rabbi Joel Sirkes ruled that:

---

[9] John D. Rayner. *Jewish Religious Law. A Progressive Perspective*. Providence: Berghan Books, 1998, p. 146.

[10] Golinkin, p. 288.

[11] Kaufmann Kohler. *Burial of Non-Jewish Wifes in Jewish Cemeteries*. In: Walter Jacob (ed.). *American Reform Responsa. Collected Responsa of the Central Conference of American Rabbis, 1889–1983*. New York: The Conference, 1983, pp. 323–335, here p. 323.

[...] in any case it is possible to bury non-Jewish dead together with Jewish dead in the same courtyard, because of the ways of peace, provided that they have been found dead together.[12]

If the whole cemetery had been holy, such a ruling would have been impossible. However a certain distance must be kept and this will be discussed as we proceed.

The saying שאין קוברין רשע אצל צדיק brings us to our next main passage that features prominently in this discussion and which creates my apologetic tendencies. So far no reason for the refusal to bury non-Jews has been given.

The connection between the burial of non-Jews and the dictum שאין קוברין רשע אצל צדיק has been introduced by the Ran in his commentary to Alfasi's summary of Git. 61a. The Ran also holds contra Rashi that one has to bury non-Jewish dead even if no Jew is to be buried. But he continues:

In any case one may not bury them (i.e. non-Jews) alongside Jews, for one does not bury a wicked person next to a righteous one, but one only tends to bury them [elsewhere].[13]

According to a *kal va-homer* argument it has to be assumed that a non-Jew is classified as a wicked person and the Jew as the righteous one. In fact this explanation has been given in many traditional responsa which are valid until the present day. It is rather obvious that this kind of assertion is unbearable to a liberal, and I would say, to any thinking Jew. Therefore we will now examine the source and its halakhic status.

This is of importance because the classification has an impact on the question, if the corpse of a wicked person is to be disinterred if buried next to a righteous one. The *Mishnah* in Sanhedrin 6:5–6 states:

[...] They did not bury him [i.e. the executed person] in his ancestral gravesite but the Bet Din instituted two cemeteries one for those who were beheaded and those who were strangled and one for those who were stoned and those who were burned. [...] If the flesh decomposed, one collects the bones and buries them in their [ancestral] place.

The *Gemara* comments this *mishnah* as follows:

Why is this necessary? Because we do not bury a wicked person next to a righteous one. For R' Acha bar Chanina says: From where [do we derive the rule] that one does not bury a wicked person next to a righteous one, for it is written [2 Kgs. 13:21f]: 'Once a man was being buried, when the people caught sight of such a band; so they threw the corpse into Elisha's grave and

---

[12] Bach to *Tur, Yoreh De'ah* §367 see *The Responsa Project. Proyekt ha-shut.* Version 14+. Ramat Gan: Bar Ilan University, 1992–2005.

[13] Ran's comment on Rif, *Gittin* 28a in: *Talmud Bavli*. Yerushalayim: Tal Man, 1981.

made of. When the [dead] man came in contact with Elisha's bones, he came to live and stood up.'[14] Rav Papa said to him: 'But maybe [the man was resurrected merely] to fulfill [Elisha's request to Elijah's]. 'Let a double portion of your spirit pass to me' [2 Kgs. 2:9]. He said to him: 'If the Baraita should have taught that he stood up and went to his house.'[15] But concerning the verse 'Let a double portion of your spirit pass to me' where do we find a case where he revived someone? R' Yochanan said to him: '[We find] that he healed Naaman's scales,[16] which is tantamount to death, for it is written [concerning Miriam who was afflicted with scales]: 'Let her not be as one dead' [Num. 12:12]. And just as one does not bury a wicked person next to a righteous one, so does one not bury a severely wicked person next to a nominally wicked person. But let them institute four cemeteries! [The institution of] two cemeteries is a received teaching.

There is considerable disagreement about the question of the halakhic status of this saying. Moses Sofer's opinion represents one side in a spectrum of possible positions. He holds that the saying שאין קוברין רשע אצל צדיק is a הלכה למשה מסיני and that it is equivalent to a biblical commandment, and in case of doubt one is stringent. His notion is based on Rashi's comment to the *mishnah*: the *Bet Din* instituted two cemeteries. Rashi says: It is explained in the *Gemara* that [the institution of] two instead of four cemeteries is a הלכה למשה מסיני.[17] However, he concludes that, even though we are dealing with a prohibition of the Torah, we must not necessarily disinter a body because the *Mishnah* states that the delinquents might be buried in their ancestral plot after the decomposition of the flesh. But as this *teshuvah* speaks about a case where the wickedness of the person is in doubt, I think we can agree with Ovadia Yosef who holds that if there is no doubt about the person's wickedness, Moses Sofer would have ruled that such person should be disinterred.[18]

But Rabbi Meshulam Rath and, in his wake, Rabbi Arusi argue that this is not necessarily the case. Rabbi Arusi has correctly observed that the two assumptions underlying this discussion are not undisputed, namely the one that claims the person thrown into Elisha's grave was a wicked one and was only revived for not being buried next to Elisha. There is a tradition in *Pirke de Rabbi Eliezer* 33 that the person who was thrown into the grave was in fact a righteous person. Concerning the latter assumption we find a discussion in the *sugya* itself.[19]

---

[14] According to Rav Aha bar Hanina the person was revived because he should not be buried next to the righteous prophet Elisha.

[15] Why did he die just after he "left" the grave?

[16] 2 Kgs. 5:1–19.

[17] Rashi on Sanh. 46a.

[18] Ovadia Yosef, *She'elot u-teshuvot, Yoreh De'ah* §36, p. 284f.

[19] Ratson Arusi. *During their Lives and their Death They Are Separated*. In: *Tehumim*, 14. Jerusalem: Zomet, Torah and Science Research Teams, Alon Shevut-Geth, 5754, p. 314; Meshullam Rath. *Kol mevaser.*

The fact that only two separate cemeteries are necessary and not four is a הלכה למשה מסיני as made clear by the Talmud itself. The principle שאין קוברין רשע אצל צדיק is based upon the verse from Kings:[20] Roth and Arusi regard it only as a rabbinic warning.

Even if the dictum is הלכה למשה מסיני it is no clear whether in case of doubt a decision has to be taken in a stringent manner though Maimonides holds the opposite.[21] More importantly, Maimonides does not mention the principle שאין קוברין רשע אצל צדיק in his *Mishneh Torah* at all.

The principle is only applied to those convicted by the Bet Din. Maimonides holds that it is not applicable to those sentenced to death by secular courts. The Maharil considers it merely as a custom.[22]

Apparently the longstanding and among orthodox Rabbis widely reproduced opinion to prohibit burying non-Jews alongside Jews is considered as a prohibition of the Torah, a notion which has been built on a one-sided reading of the sources. Even if we were to conclude, as I do, that the principle קוברין רשע אצל צדיק is only a pious recommendation, one has to realize that most of the *poskim* have ruled on it differently and declared the burial of non-Jews in a Jewish cemetery forbidden. We might have a look, if some of the orthodox *poskim* tried to provide a reason in order to smoothen the rather unethical implication that a Jew is per se a righteous person, a non-Jew a wicked one, and according to this principal a wicked Jew better than a righteous non-Jew.

Due to the vast amount of related responsa I am going to put forward only a few of those that explicitly deal with these implications.

Eliezer Deutsch of Bonyhád writes in his responsa *Peri ha-sadeh*:

[...] the Ran writes that the reason is because 'we do not bury a wicked person next to a righteous one' and the obvious implication of the Rans opinion is, that a non-Jew is not worse than a wicked [Jew] next to a righteous [Jew].[23]

She'elot u-teshuvot be-tseruf Besorot Eliyahu he'arot u-ve'urim 'al sifre ha-Gera Kol Mevasser. Yerushalayim: Mosad ha-Rav Kuk, 1972, Pt. 1 §1. See also *The Responsa Project. Proyekt ha-shut.* Version 14+. Ramat Gan: Bar Ilan University, 1992–2005.

[20] 2 Kgs. 13:21f.

[21] Mosheh ben Maimon. *Mishneh Torah. Hu ha-Yad ha-hazakah.* Yerushalayim: Wagshal, 1990, here *Hilkhot Shehita* 5:3.

[22] Ya'acov Molin. *Sefer Maharil minhagim shel Ya'acov Molin. Yotse le-or 'a. p. defusim yeshanim ve-khitve yad be-tseruf tsiyunim u-mekorot* [...] *'al yede Shelomoh Y. Shpitzer.* Yerushalayim: Mif'al Torat Hakhme Ashkenaz, Mekhon Yerushalayim, 1989, p. 602.

[23] Eliezer Deutsch. *She'elot u-teshuvot peri ha-sadeh. Zeh sefer toldot peri mahshevotai.* Paks: Rozenboim, 1905/06–1914/15, §29:3, p. 16f. For a similar statement see Aryeh Leib ben Isaac Horowitz. *Sefer She'elot u-teshuvot hare besamim. 'Al arba'ah helke ha-Shulhan 'arukh.* Lemberg: Y.M. Nik, 1883–1897, § 222, p. 140.

Following the *Sefer Gilyon Maharsha* (Solomon ben Akiva Eger) to *Yoreh Deah* 362[24] he argues that the principle שאין קוברין רשע אצל צדיק is only applicable ab initio, and that the words of the Ran proof, that no *kal va-homer* argument is intended. He thinks that the reason for the prohibition of שאין קוברין רשע אצל צדיק lies in the honor of the righteous person that might be diminished. The righteous should not see the suffering of the wicked. As this is not applicable to non-Jews, a non-Jew might be buried next to a Jew. However, in order not to shame a wicked Jew this is not to be done.

Deutsch seems to contradict himself elsewhere. In *Sefer Duda'e ha-sadeh*[25] he explains that the prohibition results from different origins of the souls of Jews and non-Jews. After the death of the body their souls take different routes to the respective place of origin. Thus it is advantageous for both that the places of burial are separated. From this assertion hence follows that one should disinter a non-Jewish dead.

Another *posek* who has dealt with this problem is Rabbi Moses Feinstein. He writes that:

> It is obvious that one does not bury a Jew next to a non-Jew even after twelve month and it follows that one does not even bury [Jews] next to Noahides who observe the seven compulsory commandments, this is not because of their (i.e. the non-Jews) wickedness, but because they do not posses of the holiness of Israel.[26]

Feinstein argues that there is a distinction between Jews and non-Jews with regard to the levels of holiness. This explanation already has been brought forward by Rabbi Kluger[27] who adds another aggadic argument to show that there must be a separation between Jewish and non-Jewish graves. It is based upon Ex. 26:33: "so that the curtain shall serve you as a partition between the Holy and the Holy of Holies."

It is rather obvious that the explanations adduced by the authorities above are by no means satisfactory and warrant an abolition of this principle. In addition it is clear from the burial practice in Germany that this principle is not observed among Jews, why then should it be observed regarding non-Jews?

---

[24] Solomon ben Akiva Eger. *Sefer Gilyon Maharsha*. In: *Shulhan 'arukh*. Tel Aviv: Tal Man, 1977, *Yoreh De'ah*, vol. 3, p. 355.

[25] Eliezer Deutsch. *Sefer Duda'e ha-sadeh*. 'Al hil. Semhot. Teshuvot [...] ve-likute dinim. Se'ini: Vi'eder, 1929, §33, p. 12f.

[26] Moses Feinstein. *Sefer Igrot Mosheh*. Nyu York: Moryah, 1959, *Yoreh De'ah* 3:146.

[27] Solomon ben Judah Aaron Kluger. *Sefer She'elot u-teschuvot Tuv ta'am va-da'at,* Vol. 2. New York: Grossman's Publ. House, § 253, p. 214.

However, all orthodox authorities agree that there needs to be at least a separation. Rabbi Golinkin has collected six different attitudes, of which he considers the following three the most preferable ones, as they are extensions of the following three: a *mehiza* or wall of 10 *tefahim* height, a hedge or fence which is at least 10 *tefahim* high, a distance of four *amot*.[28]

But if Golinkin's interpretation of the *Baraita* in *Gittin* and its parallels in the *Tosefta* and the *Yerushalmi* is correct and if we view the dictum of שאין קוברין רשע אצל צדיק as not applicable because it is ethically offensive and according to Maimonides just a pious custom applicable to persons sentenced to death by the Sanhedrin, then there is a lack of talmudic precedents permitting or forbidding the burial of non-Jews alongside Jews in a Jewish cemetery, and we do not have to bother with degrees of separation any further.

Nevertheless we are left to decide whether or not we might digress from a long standing custom of only burying Jews in a Jewish cemetery. If we do not want to draw upon kabbalistic notions like for instance the difference of souls, there is only one plausible reason beside the argument that it is a longstanding custom, namely the idea that the refusal of the burial of a non-Jewish spouse is seen as a punishment or deterrent for marrying out.

Experience teaches that people who consider marrying a non-Jew will in all likelihood not be deterred by the fact that they might not be buried side by side in a distant future. So, this argument doesn't support the combat against mixed marriages. Beyond that, there were times in which being married to a non-Jewish could have saved your life. We are morally obligated to bury those non-Jewish spouses who stood by their Jewish wives and husbands, especially when one considers that many of the non-Jewish Germans divorced their Jewish spouses and committed them to almost certain death. This is also what Leo Baeck wrote to Rabbi Nathan Levinson in 1951:

> It has been a practice, which has been approved by the Rabbinate, since decades in Berlin that non-Jewish couples, men and women, were allowed to be buried next to their spouses on our cemetery at Weissensee, if they so wished. Cases of husbands who stood bravely in darkest times by their Jewish wives and who are to be especially seen in this light and a burial should not be prohibited.[29]

One might say, of course, that the situation nowadays is different. This might be true, but on the one hand the majority of the Jewish population in Germany today originates from the former Soviet Union and very often has hardly any idea about

---

[28] Golinkin, pp. 292f.
[29] Nathan Peter Levinson. *Die Liberale Halachah*. In: *Udim*, Bd. 19, 1999, p. 143.

our traditions. And on the other hand, being married to a Jew in the FSU was also not an advantage. As these Jews grew up without any knowledge of Judaism it seems crucial to me to prevent them from undue hardships. But once a custom has been established to bury non-Jewish spouses it seems to me impossible to stop this or to re-evaluate it.

In addition I would like to point out that most of our congregations are not hostile towards non-Jewish spouses. In fact they are very well integrated. They often support their Jewish spouses in the Jewish upbringing of the children and help wherever they are needed. If we were to look for means against interfaith-marriage, we would have to refuse them voting rights and to prevent them from assuming offices in the Jewish community, deny them *aliyot* etc.

One might also mention that the question of the burial of non-Jews in a Jewish cemetery is not connected to the question of membership in a Jewish community or involvement of non-Jews in rituals, because a non-Jew doesn't get a Jewish burial. Therefore nothing that could be considered as an expression of Jewish believe is practiced in the burial of a non-Jew in a Jewish cemetery though it is true, that being buried in a Jewish cemetery is for a lot of Jews the only, post mortem, identification with Judaism.

Regarding the question of burial of non-Jews in Jewish cemeteries I would recomend to the communities that it is permissible to bury non-Jewish spouses and non-Jewish children below the age of 18 years. If there is no nameable opposition in the community against it I would rule that spouses might be buried side by side without any separation between them. But when this question is likely to create a split in the community, I would recommend a section within the Jewish cemetery where mixed-faith couples might be buried next to each other without any barrier. The section itself is separated from the other ones by the smallest barrier possible, i.e. a small hedge or a path four *amot w*ide. Furthermore the burial has to be organized by the Jewish community.

To sum up

It is permissible to bury non-Jewish spouses in a Jewish cemetery. In communities in which such a decision might cause great strife, there should be two sections within the cemetery: one for Jews and their non-Jewish spouses and the other only for Jews. The separation should preferably be achieved through a path. Within the mixed-faith burial plot no special separation is to be observed.

Samuel Joseph

Contemporary Challenges to Liberal Jewish Education

During the 1940's until his death in 1988, Joseph Schwab, professor at University of Chicago, was the leading voice studying and writing about how a curriculum actually comes into being. In 1942, as the professor in charge of writing the comprehensive examinations for the biological sciences at the university, he began to ponder the nature of curricula in general and the elements of examination questions in particular. As Chair of the Teacher Preparation for the Biological Sciences Curriculum Study Committee, he challenged the committee with thoughts such as: What are the elements of a curriculum? Where do they come from? From where do examination questions come? Eventually, Schwab came to the conclusion that curriculum writing required at least four disciplines to dialogue with one another. These disciplines, represented by human experts, deliberate with one another to create the curriculum. Without this deliberation one discipline becomes over weighted and the curriculum then is out of balance. Schwab named the four disciplines the learner, the teacher, the subject matter and the setting or milieu. Emphasize any one over the others and that discipline dominates the curriculum to the detriment, thought Schwab.

For example, when one talks about informal education, as opposed to formal education, one is usually referring to the setting. Informal education happens outside a classroom, formal inside a classroom. But the implications are larger. When we say informal education do we not also mean there are subject matter, teacher and learner implications? In an informal educational setting the milieu may also be, or dictate, the subject matter. Yet many of us have been in informal settings like camps, retreat sites, conference centers, where the learning, the subject is quite formal and the setting is much less relevant to the curriculum.

In a brief digression I would like to relate one positive informal education setting story: I was at a Jewish summer camp. One night, as the counselor turned off the lights in the cabin of 10 year old boys, the counselor said *laila tov*. He walked outside and looked up at a sky filled with millions of stars. Running back into the cabin he asked the boys to join him outside for a moment. "You know", he said, "Jewish tradition has a blessing for everything. There is even a blessing for seeing incredible things in the world like the stars. So listen and then repeat after me *barukh atah adonay, elohenu melekh ha-'olam, 'oseh ma'aseh bereshit* – Blessed are you, *adonay* our God, ruler of the universe, who makes the works of creation." Here was an example where setting, subject matter, teacher and learner met equally.

By 1973, Schwab writes that every learning episode involves four commonplaces. Commonplaces become the term now universally used by those who study Schwab. That is, there are four facets that frame every learning situation. The four commonplaces are named the learner, the teacher, the subject matter and the milieu or setting.

I am telling you about Schwab because I want to use his commonplaces as an organizing principle for this paper. Even more, for purposes of this paper, I will add a fifth commonplace, assessment. I will use Schwab's commonplaces as a template and guide as I address contemporary challenges to liberal Jewish education in diaspora.

Since North America represents such a large portion of diaspora Jewry, and there are so many interesting issues emanating from North America's Jewish community's efforts to improve Jewish education, I will use Schwab as my lens to analyze diaspora education read here as North America's experience. First, I want to paint with broad strokes a picture of what is occurring in North America related to Jewish education in general. I will not especially separate the various streams of the Jewish community, nor finely differentiate supplemental schooling from full time day schools. I want to give you a context in which a liberal Jewish education is embedded before I specifically look at the challenges facing contemporary liberal Jewish education.

In some sense we are living in a Golden Age for Jewish education in the United States. Making Jewish education better at what "it does" and who benefits from it, is at the top of the agenda for Jewish local, regional and national organizations and institutions. There are literally tens of millions of dollars being donated and allocated for all facets of Jewish education. While a short 25 years ago, Jewish education seemed to be the stepchild of the organized American Jewish community, today it is the center of the community's energies. One indicator is the dollars being spent. A review of education grants and allocations of a sampling of North American Jewish communities reveals for example that $1,200,000 is available from the San Francisco Federation for any local synagogue's education and youth programs; the Federation of New York has allocated more than $1,000,000 alone for an educational leadership initiative between Hebrew Union College's School of Education in New York and the Jewish Theological Seminary. This project is aimed at training principals of Reform and Conservative supplemental schools. The Avi Chai Foundation of Chicago and the Jewish Funder's Network has announced somewhere between $3.4 million and $4 million available as matching grants to assist families with tuition for day school education.

Money is one powerful way to assess how important Jewish education is on the North American Jewish community's agenda. Another indicator is the engagement of leaders' time reflecting on challenges they identify as facing the Jewish community in general. One only has to review the sessions at the annual General Assembly gathering of the UJA Federation of North America. Thousands of professional and lay leaders gather to look at strengthening North America's Jewish Community. Dozens and dozens of workshops, keynote speeches and plenary sessions are devoted to looking for ways to make Jewish education excellent, successful, and compelling.

In the liberal Jewish community the story is the same. In relative terms, the number of dollars and the number of engaged leaders are the same as the national efforts. Jewish education is at the top of the agenda. It was not too many years ago that the biennial meeting of the Union of American Hebrew Congregations (now the Union for Reform Judaism) was dominated by concerns for Israel, social justice, interfaith relations and outreach to the intermarried. The movement's leaders rarely mentioned Jewish educational issues in their major addresses. Sessions on Jewish education were few and usually poorly attended. While concerns of the past are still vital and are still a major portion of the biennial's program, Jewish education has moved to the forefront.

This year, for example, more than 100 educators and youth workers attended a pre-convention seminar dedicated to educating adolescents. During the biennial convention itself, there were many, many sessions about supplemental school curricula, early childhood centers, working with teachers, creating excellent adult education programs. A physical area of the convention center was devoted to the URJ's Department of Lifelong Learning giving consultation to congregations seeking help with their educational issues. The department reports that they were inundated with requests and filled all available appointment times.

I believe there are many reasons why Jewish education has moved to the top of the agenda. Though it is not the purpose of this paper to detail and analyze these reasons, I suggest that the struggle to answer the question: "Why be Jewish?" is at the center. In a North American Jewish community where so many born Jews opt for a fully secular life, totally disengaged from organized Jewish life, the organized Jewish community wants to attract these potential members. Included in the "why be Jewish"-question are many associated questions about: "How to be Jewish?" and to encourage individual Jews and their families to lead a rich, full and meaningful Jewish life. This is in response to born Jews who having been raised in a secular family now need guidance to lead a Jewish life connected to organized Jewry, which is in this case the synagogue. There are those Jews married to non-Jews where the couple decides to raise the children as Jews. Now there is the challenge of helping a Jewishly uneducated born Jew and his/her non-Jewish partner try to create a Jewish home for their children. Jonathan Woocher, CEO of the Jewish Education Service of North America, wrote that we must create:

> [...] a far more vibrant, engaging, content full Jewish life for large numbers of Jews. We seek to build communities of torah, chesed and tzedek a community characterized by openness and diversity, religious seriousness and lifelong learning.[1]

The non-Orthodox Jewish community in North America has fully imbibed the values of middle class America, along with achieving economic success. Yet along with becoming fully American, many are not connected to Jewish life and living. In certain metropolitan areas they are largely unaffiliated with synagogues and the larger Jewish community. But whether these Jews are affiliated with a synagogue or not, so many exist and feel comfortable with segments of the general surrounding culture, non-Jewish, even secular some would say. So it is this segment of the Jewish community that becomes the target of those who want to advance a vibrant, educated Jewish community. Unaffiliated and affiliated Jews of all ages and in all sorts of family configurations become a huge pool of potentiality.

The contemporary liberal Jewish community in North America faces many challenges as it tries to engage in Jewish learning. As mentioned earlier in this paper, I will examine various challenges using Schwab's frame of the learner, the teacher, the subject matter and the setting. I will also discuss issues related to synagogue supplemental schools, in former times called Sunday Schools, Reform Day Schools, early childhood programs and adult learning programs.

First, an overview by the frames:

The Learner

In all forms of supplemental Jewish schools regardless of Orthodox, Conservative or Reform, there are about 260,000 students attending today. There are around 180,000 students attending some form of day school. Based on the last study, which I published for the URJ in 1999–2000, there are more than 120,000 students, from age 6 through ages 17, attending Reform synagogue supplemental

---

[1] Jonathan Woocher. *Jewish Educational Leadership*. In: *Agenda. Jewish Education Service of North America*, vol. 16, Summer 2003, p. 2–6.

schools. Between 4,000–5,000 students are enrolled in one of 19 full time day schools affiliated with the Reform Movement in North America. There are 350 synagogue affiliated early childhood programs, sometimes called pre-schools, with over 30,000 students.

What do we know about these students, these learners? We know that more than 60% will drop out of their supplemental school programs immediately after bar/bat mitzvah. We know that 70% of supplemental schools report a need for special programs to cope with students who have attention deficit disorder or attention deficit hyperactivity disorder. At the same time, these schools have very few resources to support other special needs from loss of hearing, loss of sight and physical disabilities, to mental, emotional problems. Our schools do not have the support systems needed. Another important datum is that we believe that at least one third, if not up to a half, of the student population in our supplemental schools have a non-Jewish parent.

The data for Reform day schools and early childhood programs are not as complete. In the main, the demographics are similar to the supplemental school population. What we do not know is the number of intermarried households that send their children to a full time Jewish school.

The Teacher

In supplemental schools, the teachers overwhelmingly identify as Reform Jews. This may be a doubled edged sword. On the one side the teacher's philosophy matches that of the school's. On the other side, the teacher raised in a typical Reform religious school may not have the Judaic and Hebraic content needed to really be the best teacher.

The total population of teachers is more than 70% female and most frequently they are a parent of children in the school. They have a university bachelor's degree, but rarely is it in Jewish studies or education. This means that the teachers are well meaning and interested, but untrained both in the content of what they are teaching and in the delivery process for that content. The result is classrooms that have discipline problems, students misbehaving, and subject matter that maybe miscommunicated, taught incorrectly, not taught deeply enough.

The day schools tend to run two required learning tracks, Jewish studies, including Hebrew language instruction, and secular studies. As is the supplemental school, the teaching staff in general is primarily female and the Jewish studies teachers are almost all female. Since fulltime teachers in these schools need to be licensed by the state, the teachers all have university degrees in the areas in which they teach.

In the early childhood programs, the teachers are the youngest, most inexperienced, least paid. Many of the teachers are not Jewish. Turnover is very great.

Subject Matter

In supplemental schools, Hebrew Bible and Jewish holidays dominate the curriculum. Learning about life cycle events comes next in emphasis. Jewish history, Israel, ethics and Jewish thought, liturgy, and theology are some of the other subjects that appear sporadically in the curriculum. Supplemental schools also add extracurricular subjects throughout the course of study. These areas include *tzedakah* study, *tzedakah* projects and money collection, sometimes drama sessions, Jewish cooking, arts and crafts, reading and research in the library. Hebrew language is a separate study track, primarily devoted toward bar/bat mitzvah preparation. Students learn to decode the sounds of Hebrew letters and words in order to read from the *siddur* and the Torah. It is uncommon that students actually learn the meanings of the words, so the students read Hebrew sounds, but to the student it is untranslated and devoid of meaning.

In day schools, the secular curriculum is regulated by the state requirements. Jewish studies are up to the decision of the school. There is a strong emphasis on Hebrew language reading, writing and speaking. Hebrew language studies are a dominant feature of the day school curriculum. Not surprisingly, studying about Israel and a student trip to Israel is connected to the Hebrew language studies. Students also study Jewish texts *tanakh*, Rashi, and some rabbinic sources. The calendar of the day school follows the rhythm of the Jewish year, so the students study and celebrate Jewish holidays. Jewish history is also a subject studied during several of the years in the school. What is apparent is that because of the ability to actually teach Hebrew as a real language, day schools have the time to do so and the parents of the students expect that Hebrew is part of the curriculum. All the other facets of a Jewish studies curriculum follow and build on that fact.

Jewish holidays are the core of any so-called Jewish curriculum in early childhood centers.

Setting

Supplemental schools generally meet 25 to 30 times per school year; on Sunday morning; 2 ½ hours to 3 hours per session, around 9 am until 12 pm; from September to June. Sessions are held in synagogue classrooms.

Day schools need more classroom space than the supplemental schools, especially in the upper grades. Space for science labs, art and music rooms, and places for indoor and outdoor physical education is required. The school day in a day school is longer than the school day in general full time schools. That is because the students essentially are taking two parallel curricula, the Jewish and the secular. The day school meets five days per week, from September to June.

Local, state and federal laws regulate early childhood program's space. One of the big issues for early childhood programs is when do they begin in the morning and when do they end. If the philosophy of the school includes the notion of the program as also a day care center for working parents, the school opens early in the morning and stays open until early evening to accommodate the needs of the working parent. Some early childhood centers believe that day care is not their mandate, so they operate half-day programs 9 am until 11:30.

Having now situated liberal Jewish education in North America within the context of what is occurring in North American non-orthodox Jewish education and then looking at some of what we know about Reform supplemental schools, day schools and early childhood programs, now let us look at the challenges facing supplemental schools, day schools and early childhood centers again using Schwab's framework of the learner, the teacher, the subject matter and the setting.

Schwab asks us to look at how one commonplace can be emphasized over another and thereby become the identifier of the learning situation. For example, when I say day school versus supplemental school, I am emphasizing "setting" over the other commonplaces. We then think of learner, teacher and subject matter through the lens of setting. Setting affects how the learner and teacher interact, what we choose as subject matter and how it is delivered. Informal education versus formal education is a combination of the subject matter commonplace with the setting commonplace.

As we look at challenges to contemporary liberal Jewish education, I will again address them via each of the commonplaces. At the same time, there is this symbiosis between the commonplaces; each has implications, an affect on the other. For this paper I am discussing each area a bit more discreetly than it appears in reality. The commonplaces affect one another and therefore there is a blending, or at least some overlap.

In any case, here are the challenges as told thorough the commonplaces.

Challenges Related to the Learner

As the teenager is completing high school years, at a time when he/she is at his/her highest level of cognitive functioning since the beginning of supplemental school, schooling ends. In supplemental schools, there is rarely any program for students post bar/bat mitzvah, above the age of 13 years. Where a confirmation program exists, generally around the age of 16 years old, it may signal the end of any formal study for the child. Contemporary liberal Jewish education faces the challenge of how to be committed to our teenaged students in their last years before entering university. We need to make the formal education of this age cohort a major priority. They will need the facts, concepts, and values of Judaism in general and liberal Judaism in particular as they enter the university. Time and again we hear anecdotally that our young adults encounter more observant and knowledgeable Jews on the university campus and cannot hold their own in discussion and dialogue. Compelling, interesting, engaging and content full Jewish education for this age group is a must.

In the Reform day school realm the same challenge exists because of the 19 Reform day schools, only 3 or so have a high school program. So after six to eight years of Hebrew language instruction, the students go to a secular high school maybe never to use their Hebrew again except during *tefilah*.

Is there a place for the adult who is a Reform day school graduate in the Reform synagogue of North America? The graduate of a Reform day school finds him/herself much more Judaically and Hebraically literate than the vast majority of other members of the Reform congregation. Most of the *tefilot* and other programming in the congregation are geared toward the majority and those people tend to be much less Judaically and Hebraically educated. The Reform day school graduate may find the Reform synagogue too "dumbed down" for his/her needs and therefore decides to leave the Reform Movement for what he/she perceives as a more intense, if not traditional synagogue. We must raise the level of Jewish knowledge and practice for all congregants. The synagogue could provide alternative choices in prayer services and study sessions for those who are more knowledgeable. We do not want to lose these graduates of Reform day schools when they are adults. Of course this challenge relates directly to the challenge of life long Jewish learning, which I will address as my next point. The synagogue must have programs to raise the literacy of those less knowledgeable. Over time, maybe the graduates of day schools will find peers in the congregation. These peers were educated not in the day schools, but in the synagogue's adult programs.

How do we instill a commitment to lifelong Jewish learning? This challenge is so large that it could be a paper for this conference in and of itself. Research about the learning style, learning needs, brain functioning of adult learners is occurring at many universities in North America. With so many adults returning to universities and other training institutions for a second and third career change, this kind of research is very necessary and valuable. We also have a very large number of adults that require ongoing training and education even while remaining in their current positions.

In the Jewish world, we have a long history of valuing the adult learner. In more recent times, Buber and Rosenzweig knew that adult learning was a key value in the Jewish community and created institutions for that fact.

During the post WW II years, the Reform Movement in North America seemed very child centered educationally. Some labeled it juvenile Jewry.

Today, the Reform Movement in North America is actually doing much better at this challenge than ever before. Many different modalities are being used to capture the interest of adults to continue their Jewish study. For example, the URJ's "Ten Minutes of Torah" attracts tens of thousands of adults each week. This on-line program, together with a weekly, *parashah ha-shavua*, and study session are good examples of life long learning opportunities. The Internet itself proves to be an exceptional way for the busy adult to be involved in Jewish learning. Congregations are offering weekend study retreats, their own individualized on-line study sessions, study as part of the monthly congregational newsletter. Several congregations located around North America have purchased the copyrights to receive live video broadcasts of Jewish adult education programs from the Young Men's Hebrew Association in New York City. The technology even allows for those watching on TV to participate by emailing questions during the broadcast.

A visit to the URJ's web site linking to adult learning is interesting. There one finds many, many learning opportunities for the adult learner.

There is still much to do. The problem is our supplemental school programs do not have as one of their goals to foster a commitment to life long learning. I am not convinced that the population who currently is engaged in adult learning comes to it via their religious school experiences. A commitment to adult learning should be a core outcome for our programs that conclude with teens before entering university. At the same time, our congregations must believe in the importance of providing top flight adult learning programs as much as they believe in providing Shabbat and holiday worship.

Interfaith families are a learner frame challenge: We must learn much more about the cognitive and the affective needs of parents in interfaith families. The Reform Movement has succeeded in bringing thousands of these people to the synagogue. But typical assumptions about Jewish family life do not apply here.

We have to find out what they want and need in order to be "good parents" as they raise Jewish children. These parents become learners. We need to continue to create programs and educational support systems for this population.

Challenges Related to the Teacher

What we know about making the environment for successful teachers in a religious community is that the teachers have to teach in, participate in and create that religious community. What makes this difficult is the absence of a religious community where the teacher, the students and the students' families engage with Jewish texts as shareholders in the congregation, where they worship, celebrate, study and create together. Learning and searching together is prized. The teacher models the core values of the community; shows how to integrate religious and secular values, shows how the religious community has integrity. And, it is important that he perceives himself as a member of that community, that congregation. The teacher must be committed to a religious community and cannot just be an employee. In fact, I believe that the teacher must have a personal vision of Jewish community/congregational life.

Beyond that, how do we get better-educated teachers pedagogically, Hebraicly and Judaicly and secondly, how do we get a better training for the teachers and are subsequently able to retain them?

The recruitment, training, and retaining of our teachers in Jewish schools is a number one priority for the North American Jewish community. It is at the top of the agenda of all the relevant Jewish organizations and institutions. Everyone is trying to create a scheme that will solve the teacher shortage problem. This is a critical issue for both the supplemental schools and the day schools. No one has yet discovered the answer. But the implications are clear. We do not have enough of the right staff to teach our learners. Well meaning bodies standing in front of the class are simple unacceptable. The North American Jewish community will have to creatively find, train and keep these teachers.

Teaching special needs students: I mentioned earlier that our schools are ill equipped to deal with the many problems, physically and emotionally affecting our students. Teachers must be trained in the best ways to teach and engage students with these special needs. At this moment, these special needs students are far from getting much benefit from a Jewish education.

Principals, heads of schools are in short supply. Not surprising that hand in hand with a teacher shortage, there is a shortage of qualified people to head the schools. In past times the school would promote a veteran classroom teacher to head the school. Many times this was a mistake. Because one was good as a classroom teacher did not necessarily mean that that person could lead and manage a school. Also, by moving that teacher out of the classroom, the students lost the benefit of that teacher's skills and knowledge

Outside of the few graduate training institutions, like HUC, who prepare educational leaders to head schools, there are very few ways heads of schools can get the training and the mentoring needed to become successful. This is also a very important challenge to North American Jewish education.

Challenges Related to the Subject Matter

The last time goals of education for the Reform Movement were written and revisited was almost 30 years ago. It is time to revisit this issue. It directly relates to challenges facing us out of the subject matter frame. What do our students need in order to live a meaningful, rich liberal Jewish life? What do they need to know? What skills do they need?

Goals are needed that are related to the values, knowledge and skills one needs to live a liberal Jewish life. As I mentioned, the goals are now almost 30 years old. Some need to be rethought. While none of them is so out of step today as to be that problematic, a few goals could stand some reflection.

- Jews who affirm their Jewish identity and bind themselves inseparably to their people by word and deed.
- Jews who bear witness to the *brit* (the covenant between God and the Jewish people) by embracing Torah through study and observance of the *mitzvot* (commandments) as interpreted in the light of historic development and contemporary thought.
- Jews who affirm their historic bond to *Eretz Yisrael*, the Land of Israel.
- Jews who cherish and study Hebrew, the language of the Jewish people.
- Jews who value and practice *tefilah* (prayer).
- Jews who further the causes of justice, freedom and peace by pursuing *tzedek* (righteousness), *mishpat* (justice), and *hesed* (loving deeds).
- Jews who celebrate Shabbat and the festivals and observe the Jewish ceremonies marking the significant occasions in their lives.
- Jews, who esteem their own person and the person of others; their own community and the community of others.
- Jews who express their kinship with *Kelal Yisrael* by actively seeking welfare of Jews throughout the world.
- Jews who support and participate in the life of the synagogue.

Teaching Israel is a requirement. But what to teach about Israel and how to teach Israel is a challenge. Should Israel be taught for the purpose of helping the student choose to make *aliyah*? Why teach Israel? Certainly this is a challenge out of the subject matter frame.

In the liberal setting prayer is a big challenge. How should we teach prayer? How can we educate in order to create a habit of prayer? Can prayer be taught in a one-day-a-week school? Can prayer be taught in a synagogue's supplemental school where the synagogue itself puts little emphasis on prayer? These are just two of the many questions surrounding this subject matter issue.

It is very important to note that the URJ's Department of Learning is engaged in a multi year project of creating a new curriculum for supplemental schools. Called the *Chai* Curriculum, it is grounded in the most recent of educational research. It is being written, professional piloted, edited and evaluated. Along with the *Chai* Curriculum, the URJ is writing a Hebrew curriculum called *Mitkadem*. It, too, is part of a writing, editing, piloting and evaluation process. What is groundbreaking about *Mitkadem* is that it is meant to be self paced, with a teacher. There are 23 levels, so students of various backgrounds are able to find their way into the material.

One brief mention of another challenge related to subject matter. We have not done a very good job using the arts, both the plastic and the performative, as part of Jewish education. There is obviously a huge world of possibilities in this area.

Challenges Related to Setting

When I think of the setting frame, I am reminded of a program run by the Philadelphia schools in the 1960's. Along a major street in Philadelphia, called the Benjamin Franklin Parkway, there are several important educational, scientific, cultural and research institutions. Using this street as a base, students could attend the Parkway School. All their work occurred in or about these institutions the public library's main branch, the Museum of Natural History, the Franklin Institute of Science, The Art Museum, the Rodin Museum, etc. Setting was clearly the key.

We have the historical knowledge to know that Sunday mornings, in the synagogue classrooms, three hours per session, is the neither only, nor optimal place and time for Jewish learning. The success of camps, retreats and the like show that there are other settings that can work educationally. We should have learned the setting lesson a long time ago.

Israel can be a very successful setting for learning. Once one's goals are clear about what one wants to accomplish in Israel, the setting can be the driving force.

Other travels to Jewish communities, places and sites around the world can be excellent settings for Jewish learning outside the four walls of a classroom as well.

Even the home itself as an educational setting can be powerful. Some have said, and I agree, that the home is the most important setting. We have not done far enough in using this setting as a place for real Jewish education. Instead, we see the home as a place where the learner either catches "Jewish" or not. Like someone catching a cold.

The challenge facing us is how to best choose and utilize settings outside the classroom and then match the subject frame to the setting. The setting frame is very connected to the subject frame.

Evaluation Frame

I am going to mention a fifth frame, one that Schwab did not discuss. This is the evaluation frame. We are in great need of requiring assessment of our educational programs. We need both quantitative and qualitative assessment, related to our goals. At this point we have little or no way of knowing if we are achieving anything in our programs. So evaluation, assessment is a vital challenge.

Summary

Looking at challenges facing the North American Jewish Community, one can see that there are many. The good is that there is a will, a desire to improve. This by itself is more than existed just a few decades ago. People really do want to meet the challenges. I am optimistic actually.

I am also interested in how other Diaspora Jewish communities are wrestling with similar and different challenges of Jewish education. One should not construe my paper as implying in any way that the North American experience is the most important experience from which to judge and model. On the contrary, I want to strongly advise to look toward the North American experience only to learn how not to reinvent the wheel whether that wheel is square or round. In other words, other communities will create, out their own cultural norms and assumptions, educational programs and projects that they believe are successful or not. We all may find strength and success in some cross cultural partnerships. In the end we are all dedicated to creating an educationally knowledgeable Jewish community.

Contributors

Prof. Dr. Ernst Ludwig Ehrlich
Professor DDr. Ernst Ludwig Ehrlich is Honorary Vice President of B'nai B'rith Continental Europe and a Senator of the Abraham Geiger College. He studied at the Berlin Hochschule für die Wissenschaft des Judentums, his teacher was Leo Baeck.

Rabbi Dr. Walter Homolka
Rabbi Dr. Walter Homolka is Principal of Abraham Geiger College at the University of Potsdam, Chairman of the Leo Baeck Foundation and a Member of the Executive Board of the World Union for Progressive Judaism. He is engaged in the Jewish-Christian dialogue forum of the Central Committee of German Catholics.

Rabbi Prof. Samuel Joseph
Rabbi Samuel Joseph is Professor of Jewish Education and Leadership Development at Hebrew Union College-Jewish Institute of Religion in Cincinnati, Ohio. His specialties are synagogue leadership development, curriculum development and adult education. In 2006, he was the Walter Jacob Jubilee Fellow at the Abraham Geiger College at the University of Potsdam.

Rabbi Dr. Dalia Marx
Rabbi Dr. Dalia Sara Marx teaches Liturgy and Midrash at Hebrew Union College Jerusalem and at the Hebrew University. She is engaged in research of textual, historical and theological as well as Anthropological aspects of Jewish ritual and prayer. Rabbi Marx was the 2005 Walter Jacob Jubilee Fellow at the Abraham Geiger College at the University of Potsdam.

Prof. Dr. Michael A. Meyer
Prof. Dr. Michael A. Meyer is Adolph S. Ochs Professor of Jewish History at Hebrew Union College-Jewish Institute of Religion in Cincinnati and International President of the Leo Baeck Institute. He is specialized in Jewish intellectual history and the history of Reform Judaism.

Thomas Rachel
Thomas Rachel is a Member of the German Parliament, Parliamentary State Secretary to the Ministry of Education and Research, Federal Chairman of the Protestant Group of the Christian Democratic Party and a Trustee of the Leo Baeck Foundation.

Dr. Esther Seidel
Dr. Esther Seidel is Senior Lecturer for Jewish Philosophy at Leo Baeck College London and co-editor of the journal European Judaism. Her field of research is the Jewish intellectual history and the Hochschule für die Wissenschaft des Judentums.

Rabbi Jonah Sievers
Rabbi Jonah Sievers is Rabbi of the Jewish Congregation Braunschweig and Secretary of the General Rabbinic Conference of the Central Council of Jews in Germany (Allgemeine Rabbinerkonferenz des Zentralrats der Juden in Deutschland). His special expertise is modern halakhah.

Appendix

DR. WOLFGANG SCHÄUBLE, MdB
Bundesminister des Innern

Bundesministerium des Innern
Alt-Moabit 101 D
10559 Berlin

Frau
Marianne C. Dreyfus
Nine Prospect Park West # 11
BROOKLYN, N.Y. 11215 – 1741
USA

Berlin, den 31. Oktober 2006

Sehr geehrte Frau Dreyfus,

in diesen Tagen erinnern wir an den Tod von Rabbiner Dr. Leo Baeck, Ihres Großvaters, vor 50 Jahren am 2. November 1956. Wir erinnern damit an den „großen Lehrer und Leiter des Judentums", als den ihn sein Biograph Albert Friedlander gewürdigt hat, und an den Rabbiner, der seine Gemeinde in der Stunde ihrer größten Not nicht verlassen wollte und deshalb von den nationalsozialistischen Machthabern in das Konzentrationslager und Ghetto Theresienstadt deportiert wurde.

„Wer immer in unserer Mitte wohnt, soll nicht bloß räumlich neben uns leben, sondern mit uns leben".

100 Jahre sind vergangen, seitdem Leo Baeck diesen Satz über den Mitmenschen formuliert hat. Von Anfang an galt er nicht nur der Begegnung und dem Gespräch zwischen Juden und Christen, sondern umfasste – ganz im Sinne der ethischen Grundsätze, denen sich Leo Baeck Zeit seines Lebens verpflichtet wusste – alle Religionen und Minderheiten. Die Ausgrenzung von Menschen und Minderheiten fängt oftmals mit der religiösen Frage an. Leo Baeck hat dem die Aufforderung entgegengesetzt „In unserer Mitte leben, mit uns leben" und dies auch selbst gelebt, etwa in der Seelsorge im Konzentrationslager für Menschen unterschiedlichen Glaubens.

Leo Baeck, sein Denken und sein Handeln, haben in den vergangenen Jahrzehnten Juden und Christen in Deutschland und weltweit zum Dialog sowie zum Glaubensgespräch zusammengeführt.

Gegenwärtig sind wir Zeugen einer erstarkten, lebendigen und weiter wachsenden jüdischen Gemeinschaft in unserem Land. Die Rabbinerordinationen vor wenigen Wochen in Dresden, die ersten in Deutschland nach der Shoah, und die bevorstehende Einweihung der neuen Synagoge in München sind dafür hoffnungsfrohe Zeichen und ein Grund zur Dankbarkeit. Ich möchte damit auch die Erinnerung verbinden, dass es Leo Baeck war, der nach dem Ende von Krieg und Katastrophe Juden in Deutschland Hoffnung und Zuversicht zusprach.

In Dankbarkeit für das bleibende Vermächtnis von Leo Baeck grüße ich Sie freundlich

Translation

Marianne C. Dreyfus
Nine Prospect Park West # 11
BROOKLYN, N.Y. 11215 – 1741
USA

Berlin, 31 October 2006

Dear Mrs Dreyfus,

In these days we commemorate the death of your grandfather, Rabbi Dr. Leo Baeck, who died 50 years ago on 2 November 1956. We recall the "great teacher and leader of Judaism" as Albert Friedlander, his biographer, called him paying tribute to him, and we recall the rabbi who refused to leave the members of his community in their darkest hour and was therefore deported by the Nazis to Theresienstadt.

"Wer immer in unserer Mitte wohnt, soll nicht bloß räumlich neben uns leben, sondern mit uns leben" (Whoever lives in our midst should not merely live aside of us, but with us).

A hundred years have passed since Leo Baeck formulated this sentence about how human beings should live together. From the beginning it was meant to apply not only to Jews and Christians, but – fully in line with the ethical principles Leo Baeck subscribed to throughout his life – to all religions and minorities. The marginalization of people and minorities often begins with the question of religion. Against this Leo Baeck not only set his appeal "live in our midst, live with us", but he also lived it, for example with his spiritual welfare work for people of different faiths in the concentration camp.

During the past decades, Leo Baeck, his thoughts and actions have brought together Jews and Christians in Germany and the world over to enter into a dialogue and to discuss religion.

At the moment we are witnessing the emergence of a vibrant and growing Jewish community in our country. The ordination of rabbis a few weeks ago in Dresden – the first rabbis to be ordained in Germany since the Shoah – and the imminent consecration of the new synagogue in Munich are hopeful signs of this development and give us every reason to be grateful. In this context I would also like to recall that it was Leo Baeck who, after the war and the Holocaust, gave hope and comfort to Jews in Germany.

With gratitude for the lasting legacy of Leo Baeck I remain

Yours sincerely,

Dr. Wolfgang Schäuble
Minister of the Interior of the Federal Republic of Germany

Marianne C. Dreyfus
9 Prospect Park West
Brooklyn, New York 11215
718-638-1797
E-mail: Ravstan@verizon.net

November 9, 2006

Dr. Wolfgang Schaeuble, Md.B
Bundesminister des Innern
Alt-Moabit 101 D
10559 Berlin
Germany

Dear Dr. Schaeuble:

In behalf of my husband, Rabbi Dr. A. Stanley Dreyfus, and myself, please accept our profound appreciation for your moving tribute upon the fiftieth anniversary of the death of my grandfather, Rabbi Dr. Leo Baeck, and for your eloquent portrayal of his ministry to Jews and non-Jews whom he served and helped to endure the persecutions visited upon them by their inhumane oppressors. Leo Baeck taught them, interceded for them with their jailors, and strengthened their faith in the power of the human spirit to defy the cruelty of tyrants, and to work toward the establishment of a just and compassionate society.

Would that this Rabbi might have lived to see the renaissance of Jewry in Germany, the founding of the Abraham Geiger Seminary for the education of rabbis, the building of new synagogues and schools and vibrant communities, all of which were not so long ago dismissed as impossible dreams. Instead they have demonstrated the invincibility of hope and the power of righteousness. May the legacy of Leo Baeck long prevail for good in the land which could not silence him.

Yours sincerely,

Marianne C. Dreyfus

AUS RELIGION UND RECHT

Band 1 Walter Homolka: Liturgie als Theologie. Das Gebet als Zentrum im jüdischen Denken. 182 Seiten. ISBN 978-3-86596-008-5

Band 2 Cristina Fernández Molina: Katholische Gemeinden anderer Muttersprache in der Bundesrepublik Deutschland. Kirchenrechtliche Stellung und pastorale Situation in den Bistümern im Kontext der europäischen und deutschen Migrationspolitik. 540 Seiten. ISBN 978-3-86596-016-0

Band 3 Péter Erdő: Kirchenrecht im mittelalterlichen Ungarn. Gesammelte Studien. 240 Seiten. ISBN 978-3-86596-028-3

Band 4 Wilhelm Handschuh: Diözesane Schieds- und Schlichtungsstellen in der katholischen Kirche. Eine rechtssystematische Untersuchung für den Bereich der Deutschen Bischofskonferenz. 260 Seiten. ISBN 978-3-86596-065-8

Band 5 Walter Homolka / Esther Seidel (Hg.): Nicht durch Geburt allein. Übertritt zum Judentum. 260 Seiten. ISBN 978-3-86596-079-5

Band 6 Walter Jakob / Walter Homolka (eds.): Hesed and Tzedakah. From Bible to Modernity. 108 Seiten. ISBN 978-3-86596-090-0

Band 7 Axel Azzola: Recht, Freiheit und Bündnis in der Tora. Grundlegungen für eine jüdische systematische Theologie. 142 Seiten. ISBN 978-3-86596-094-8

Band 8 Ronny Raith: Verwaltungsermessen im Kanonischen Recht. 202 Seiten. ISBN 978-3-86596-078-8

Band 9 Walter Homolka (ed.): Leo Baeck – Philosophical and Rabbinical Approaches. 130 Seiten. ISBN 978-3-86596-115-0

Frank & Timme

AUS RELIGION UND RECHT

Band 10 Anja Kurths: Shoahgedenken im israelischen Alltag. Der Umgang mit der Shoah in Israel seit 1948 am Beispiel der Gedenkstätten Beit Lohamei HaGetaot, Yad Vashem und Beit Terezin. 282 Seiten. ISBN 978-3-86596-177-8

Band 12 Alexander Lungu: Der in Canon 1103 des Codex Iuris Canonici von 1983 enthaltene Ehenichtigkeitsgrund. 80 Seiten. ISBN 978-3-86596-217-1

Band 13 Burkhard Josef Berkmann: Von der Blasphemie zur „hate speech"? Die Wiederkehr der Religionsdelikte in einer religiös pluralen Welt. 130 Seiten. ISBN 978-3-86596-220-1

Band 14 Szabolcs Anzelm Szuromi: From a reading book to a structuralized canonical collection. The Textual Development of the Ivonian Work. 200 Seiten. ISBN 978-3-86596-256-0

Band 15 Friedrich Lotter: Rabbiner Ignaz Maybaum – Leben und Lehre. Die Grundlagen jüdischer Diasporaexistenz. 202 Seiten. ISBN 978-3-86596-276-8

Band 16 Joachim Rott: „Ich gehe meinen Weg ungehindert geradeaus". Dr. Bernhard Weiß (1880–1951). Polizeivizepräsident in Berlin. Leben und Wirken. 224 Seiten. ISBN 978-3-86596-307-9

Band 17 Marie Vachenauer: Der Fall Simon Abeles. Eine kritische Anfrage an die zugänglichen Quellen. 270 Seiten. ISBN 978-3-86596-325-3

Band 18 Szabolcs Anzelm Szuromi: Pre-Gratian Medieval Canonical Collections. Texts, Manuscripts, Concepts. 156 Seiten. ISBN 978-3-7329-0108-1

Frank & Timme

Verlag für wissenschaftliche Literatur